Chris Leonard has written for both children and adults – mainly biographies and devotional works. She is the author of *Leaning Towards Easter*, published by SPCK in 2005 and this is her seventeenth published book. She contributes regular Bible-reading notes and also enjoys leading creative-writing courses and holidays. Her writing and teaching spring from lifelong faith, love of drawing out all the good things that are in people, and a degree in English and theology. She is married with two grown-up children and lives in Surrey. Her website is at <www.chris-leonard-writing.co.uk>.

WAITING

Reflections, Stories, Prayers

Chris Leonard

First published in Great Britain in 2008

Society for Promoting Christian Knowledge
36 Causton Street
London SW1P 4ST

The author and publisher have made every effort to ensure that
the external website and email addresses included in this book are
correct and up to date at the time of going to press. The author and
publisher are not responsible for the content, quality or continuing
accessibility of the sites.

Unless stated otherwise, scripture quotations are taken from
the HOLY BIBLE, NEW INTERNATIONAL VERSION,
Copyright © 1973, 1978, 1984 by International Bible Society.
Used by permission of Hodder & Stoughton Ltd,
a member of the Hodder Headline Plc Group.

British Library Cataloguing-in-Publication Data
A catalogue record for this book is available from the British Library

ISBN 978–0–281–05891–4

1 3 5 7 9 10 8 6 4 2

Typeset by Graphicraft Ltd, Hong Kong
Printed in the UK by CPI Bookmarque, Croydon, CR0 4TD

Produced on paper from sustainable forests

Contents

Acknowledgements

———◆◆◆———

The following people kindly gave permission to use their stories and/or poems which you will find in the sections indicated.

Introduction

Elaine Arnold, Alison Walton

His timing, our timing

Kathy Barnes, Penny Clarke, Ann Hallson, Gill Hawkins, Jan King, Ann Stringer

Waiting for

Pam Annison, Rosie Berry, Yvonne Done, Lindsay Duncombe, Helene Elston, Brigitte Furze, Jenny Goddard, Sylvia Herbert, Amanda Hoskins, Stephanie Hüsler, Margaret Legg, Tricia Phillips, Pat Price-Tomes, Sue Shaw, Ann Watts, Sarah Williams

Waiting as

Noel Allsup, Janet Catsaras, Hilary Creed, Debra Elsdon, Paula Felstead, Mary Hobbs, Rachel Gilbert, Marina Jurjevic, Eric Leat, Mary Mills, Colin Raynor, Jane Terry

Waiting on or at

Marjorie Kiddle, Ruth Walker, Lewis Wallace, Tom Wettern

Waiting on God

Jan Berry, Dorothy Gardiner, Rachel Kamara

After waiting

Roma Bell, Veronica Heley, Eric Leat, June Newcombe, Dorrith Sim, Geoff Tothill

Unattributed poems are by the author.

Introduction

Holy Island on holiday

Dry, we queue for ice creams;
field-crops of cars
grow heat and fumes.
What has happened to you,
Lindisfarne?

His determined fingers numbed
by penetrating winds,
slowly the holy hermit penned
precision through the mist,
when mist alone could reach
this place with any ease.

Pilgrims prepared to pay the price
and find the way might understand,
but we rush there
and back this afternoon,
bringing our clutter, gaining
only a foul mood.

We leave before the tide
rises and shuts us in,
hoping it makes this isle
half holy again.

Waiting makes a rich theme for a book because we all have
plenty of experience of waiting for something, or someone –
or of failing to wait, as my family did on that brief summer-
holiday afternoon trip to the Holy Island of Lindisfarne.
Waiting affects our lives and emotions so much.

Our culture leads us to expect 'instant everything' – instant credit, instant information on broadband, instant email, mobile phones, digital photography. Our ever faster, 24/7 goal-orientated 'developed' society doesn't help us to wait well, even if it's only for something like a train or plane. Churches may encourage people to 'run the race' and rush about doing all kinds of good things. They are not always taught about waiting – whether that be enforced, perhaps through an illness caused by all that stress, or strategic: Jesus drew aside to be alone with his Father; God held judgement's fire to give people more time to turn back to him. Yet isn't the world designed to run on a finely tuned balance between waiting and action? A bird which flies in a matter of weeks from South Africa to Scotland starts life being incubated inside an egg.

Have you ever waited when you should have taken action or leapt into something when you should have waited? Perhaps, like comedy, waiting is all in the timing – and the attitude. Do you find waiting exciting, frustrating, frightening, boring, interminable . . . ? Are you too restless to stay still? Do you see waiting times as investment, or robbery? Have you ever felt you were waiting at a confusing crossroads, or alone and precarious on the edge of somewhere, someone, something . . . ?

What about after we've waited, when we get what we want – or fail to do so? How do we move forward from there – and do we see the waiting period any differently when we look back?

And then there's waiting on God – how do we do that? Many times in the Bible we read about his waiting – and most of us have experienced his acting rather less quickly than we would have liked. Is it possible to learn to move to his 'different' rhythms of waiting and action, when he exists outside of time? One of our days could be like a thousand years to him, while a moment will suffice to scatter suns in the sky. For him our 'yesterday' co-exists with 4000 AD . . . or BC. The whole subject of waiting throws up so many questions which can't have definitive answers because we're following someone who exists in a dimension outside space–time – that's the challenge. The encouragement is that Jesus has also entered fully into our world, and so understands us; his message isn't complicated.

Over a couple of years I asked many 'ordinary' people, most but not all Christians, to tell me one experience they've had of waiting. I would like to thank each one because those varied stories have been one of the joys of writing this book. All the stories are true, though occasionally names have been changed. Before we fall into the daily pattern of the rest of the book, here are a couple for you to enjoy.

I love this memory from Elaine Arnold, who grew up in Barbados. Young children play outside during the warm, light evenings of English summers: in winter months when dark falls well before bedtime, it's normally too cold in the UK to play outside. But Elaine writes of waiting for magical moonlight:

My childhood was carefree and enjoyable, full of outdoor activities. Electricity had not yet reached us and so we could not always go out in the evenings to play, but at the first sight of the new moon our spirits lifted, for soon it would be First Quarter. When the Full Moon followed in all its glory everything seemed to glisten and be made new in the silvery light.

During the 'moonlight season', as we called it, our fear of walking the unlit streets would disappear and as soon as the moon rose we would set off, taking it in turns to go to each other's houses where we played on the front steps, if there was no front garden. When we needed more space for running or dancing we'd take to the road which was empty of traffic. No fear of pollution or of being run over in those days! Sometimes we would go for long walks, returning exhausted but reluctant to leave the moon to go to bed, as we knew that too soon she would disappear and the long wait would begin until the next moonlit night.

Physicists may work out complex theories and formulae concerning time but all of us experience it subjectively. It passes at different rates, especially if we're waiting. Technology consultant Alison Walton writes of her less-than-blissful boarding-school days:

They say time flies when you're enjoying yourself. Well, time grinds to a halt when you're waiting desperately for something to happen. As with watching the proverbial kettle, it seems that ringed date on the calendar will never arrive.

End of term at a boarding school has a special significance missing at a day school. An enormous pair of gates in a towering wall are grinding open, infinitesimally slowly. A glimmer of hope is filtering through; freedom is beckoning.

I draw up my end-of-term chart some weeks before D- (for Departure-) Day and carefully fill in a block with a different colour each day. The rainbow line snakes slowly to the edge of the page, then creeps down to start a new row.

The teachers continue with their lessons, droning on with physics experiments, Latin declensions, interminable maths exercises. Apparently unmoved by the pent-up anticipation of their charges, they are incredulous that we might want to get away from their hallowed classrooms. We welcome bedtimes because the hours flash by as we lie comatose in our dormitory cubicles. As each new day dawns, there's another block to colour in.

At last the interminable waiting is over. Trunks and suitcases emerge, to be filled with a higgledy-piggledy muddle of dirty clothes, odd shoes and (for the well-intentioned ones) homework books. The hall slowly clears as, one by one, we are collected by family, friends or taxis. I don't mind being last, sitting on my trunk in an empty hall – there's the final, delicious realization that the end of term has actually arrived. That's probably the best feeling of the whole holidays!

How to read this book

After the introduction you'll find the rest of the book arranged in units which are undated but you might find it helpful to read one per day. Each contains a passage from Scripture with a few words about it, a true story and/or a simple poem and a short prayer or meditation. Waiting is a huge subject and the book is divided into the following broad sections: His timing, our timing; Waiting *for* . . . ; Waiting *as* . . . ; Waiting *on* or *at* . . . ; Waiting on God; and After waiting. Most of these have sub-sections, for example Waiting *for*: something good, something bad, the unknown, one another, a very long time.

Don't rush through the book. Each 'day' is complete in itself. Take your time, enjoy, learn from other people's experience, from Scriptures written many centuries ago and from the Holy Spirit who takes cold print and, in his own time, turns it into fire, water, breeze, hurricane or whatever each individual and community need.

All Bible references are from the NIV unless stated otherwise.

His timing, our timing

Waiting to find . . .

Follow the star . . . the cloud . . . the fire
high, higher, until they come to rest,
perhaps over the place where the child is.
There discover . . . everything, and nothing, new.
Your quiet life unsettled, unsettling,
grow there, know . . . wait . . . be . . .
always ready to move on.

Seed and dough, time and tide

Listen! A farmer went out to sow his seed. As he was scattering the seed, some fell along the path, and the birds came and
ate it up. Some fell on rocky places, where it did not have much
soil. It sprang up quickly, because the soil was shallow. But when
the sun came up, the plants were scorched, and they withered
because they had no root. Other seed fell among thorns, which
grew up and choked the plants, so that they did not bear grain.
Still other seed fell on good soil. It came up, grew and produced
a crop, multiplying thirty, sixty, or even a hundred times.

(Mark 4.3–8)

A man went out to sow some wheat seed one afternoon and
the next morning, feeling hungry, he returned to check how it
was doing. What, no crop yet? Bare soil, not a trace of green,
no sign that anything had happened at all – what a lot of hard
work and fuss for nothing! The field hadn't been cheap, nor the
nitrate fertilizer! He'd taken great care to follow the instructions

1

on the packet. Perhaps he should sue someone – the seed company or the field's last owner? Meanwhile, why not jet off to some nice warm place where the fruit dropped off the trees into your lap – or simply pop down to the supermarket for a loaf? Who, these days, had time for the risky business of sowing, reaping, threshing, kneading, waiting for the dough to rise and, finally, baking?

The story Jesus told sounds OK for its time, perhaps, but not for our 'developed' world, where we expect everything instantly, if not sooner. We can pick a plastic-wrapped loaf off the shelves of a supermarket that's open 24/7 – and pay for it with plastic too. But does it satisfy our real hunger? Is it good for us? Nature's rhythms can follow slow beats and variable time signatures. Yet while nature's everyday miracles include multiplying 'up to a hundred times' and never running out, our love of speed and everything plastic consumes finite resources. If Jesus had anything to do with the way our planet – and human beings – were constructed, maybe we need to pay more attention to his stories and to the places in which he told them (in this case, on Galilee's shore). 'Time and tide wait for no man,' says the proverb. Like it or not, waiting is a part of the way this world works – and that goes for the way we, as well as plants and large bodies of water, 'tick'.

Retired hospital data manager Ann Stringer writes about letting the sweeping emotional tides following bereavement come in their own time.

> The neap tide inches inexorably up the shore. Every day it reaches a higher level on the sand and slowly, so slowly, leaves the sadness further behind.
>
> The loneliness and the longing will always be there but every time I laugh, share an experience or, as Jane Austen would say, am 'exceedingly diverted', another wave of optimism rides

up the beach. For every wave that edges forward, one returns, though not quite as far as the wave before.

The tide will not be rushed. It has its own rhythm. It is a neap tide. A spring tide goes too far, too quickly – would flood me completely, as an excess of optimism collapsed into despair.

Last year, a few months after my husband died, I went to South Africa on my own – a great adventure but too much too soon. I saw amazing animals and exotic scenery but the grinding poverty, the AIDS . . . I felt so helpless. Overwhelmed with emotion, I collapsed – but I learned about myself in South Africa. God taught me a valuable lesson. The tide will not be rushed.

This year I visited Ecuador and the Galapagos Islands with cousins – another exciting adventure but how much more enjoyable and comfortable, being with people who loved me.

The tide has come in steadily, so the shore ahead is not as daunting now. I know that I can live on my own most of the time and yet have enjoyed the company of my family – a taped telephone message from Mark aged four saying, 'I hope you are all right, Grandma Ann – love you!'; watching the International Rowing at Dorney Lake on my birthday – both grandmas jumping up and down with our boys when England won two gold medals; cheering for my football team at Stamford Bridge with my younger son, loving the passion and the drama of it; at a gig with my daughter hearing dodgy musicians dedicate a song to me. It was called 'Over the hill'. Each laugh, each shared experience, each diversion, each hand of bridge won, each shout for Chelsea sends that wave further up the beach.

A diagnosis of breast cancer two months ago revealed unexpected rocks on my beach – two operations and now chemotherapy. At least I don't have to keep my unwell husband steady while picking my way round them. Laughter brings unexpected clearings in the rocks – like when my dog ran around the lawn with my prosthetic breast in front of the postman or when Mark told me that I was going to have some really nasty medicine that would make my hair fall out. 'Grandma Ann – you will have to wear a wig!' I was – and he didn't know!

My friends have carried me through many rocky times – every day a card, some flowers, a phone call, a lunch left on the door-step after my chemotherapy, a letter from an old school-friend that lights up my morning. My church is such a refuge – on Sundays I do not have to plan my day yet know it will be full of fellowship and love.

My younger son's wedding in a few weeks will be another surge forward of the waves in our lives but we will all be prepared for the returning wave. The wave that whispers, 'Dad is not here.'

Yet we will climb this beach – whatever the tide. It will become plain sand again. The sea will draw closer to the sea wall and who knows – soon I might be able to deal with a spring tide.

Lord, I would really like there to be short cuts for Ann and others like her. I'm not a little angry with you that she has to go through such tough treatment for cancer on top of everything else the recent months have thrown at her. But your ways are not our ways, your time isn't our time. Thank you that you do sustain her. She hasn't lost her sense of humour, or her faith in and gratefulness to you. Thank you that she can feed on the words of others who have already walked this hard path with you, for the bright surges forward and for the sense that, dreadful though many things are, there is purpose. She says that she is growing as a person, 'In order to understand and help others better.' Whether we're concerned with individuals who suffer or with the ills of our planet, help us to learn to wait for you. Even when they take us to painful and rocky places, help us to move according to your tides and rhythms and to thrive according to your cycles of growth.

*   *   *

A God who waits

I tell you the truth, unless a grain of wheat falls to the ground and dies, it remains only a single seed. But if it dies, it produces many seeds. The man who loves his life will lose it, while the man who hates his life in this world will keep it for eternal life. Whoever serves me must follow me; and where I am, my servant also will be. My Father will honour the one who serves me.   (John 12.24–26)

Following Jesus, following God, means exactly that. If his ways and character involve service, we follow him by serving. If he waits – and he does, often – then we wait. Waiting on him at the same time as we wait for something is much better than waiting for it in frustration or bitterness. So . . . seeds are planted and take a while to germinate – and even longer to grow into mature plants such as trees. Babies are born a good while after conception – though thank God women don't have to wait as long as elephants! Mountain ranges take an age to rise up and even longer to wear down again. God has all the time in the world.

Jesus talks of fruitfulness coming from the 'death' of a seed. To his contemporaries, desperately poor and hungry, it must have been hard to bury something edible in the ground and risk waiting till it bore fruit – and yet they knew enough about farming to realize they would be even more hungry the next year if they ate all the seed corn immediately rather than sowing it.

I heard a story the other day of a biologist who, observing a butterfly's struggles to emerge from its chrysalis, decided to lend it a hand. Using his penknife, carefully he cut a hole through which a beautiful butterfly emerged. But within a few minutes it had fallen to the ground, dead. It needed the struggle to help pump up its wings and give it strength.

Maybe God has designed things so that something happens in the waiting – be that waiting for food, for a promised land, for a return from exile, for God to act . . . People learn to trust God at such times. In the struggle they grow. Or they turn away from God and wither.

Gill Hawkins, a Baptist minister, writes:

Having been married for three years, in 1994 Phil and I boldly decided to have a child. Our initial expectation that I'd fall pregnant faded as the weeks passed. The weeks became months and the months years until, after much agonizing about why God wouldn't just 'do it without doctors', we saw a doctor. He recommended infertility treatment. Though concerned about the ethics of it all, we went ahead. It was unsuccessful and in 2000, as I was leaving my career in midwifery and entering the ministry, we took a break from the treatment.

A roller coaster of emotion accompanied those months and years. The intoxicating hope of becoming pregnant contrasted with the desperate realization that I was not made for a challenging time. Phil's pain needed space too – and that of our parents, friends and family. It's one thing to trust God with your own pain but quite another to trust him with that of your loved ones.

Constantly holding up my request to a silent God and fumbling my way through this unexpected experience was a painful and sad time. My desire was so strong that I convinced myself several times that I had physical signs of pregnancy and even bought bootees on one occasion. Desire is such a powerful thing.

I had a sense that I was waiting and that God would give me a child – but waiting, I realized, contained a choice. I could wait well or I could wait badly. At each turn I found that there was a way. The better way always meant me facing my pain, even embracing it. God's grace was always full, even when he quietly insisted that his grace was sufficient, though I remained forever childless. Contemplating our future without children and accepting that God's grace would be enough for me was the hardest of all times.

At the end of January 2002 I found I was pregnant and the following September I had a baby boy. We called him Harry Samuel. He is now joined in all his fun by a sister named Evie Grace, born in July 2004. They are a great joy and my struggle is a distant memory.

I'm an extrovert, generally very transparent and I'd imagined many times what I'd do when I found I was pregnant: I'd cry, scream, run out into the street shouting, 'I'm pregnant!' In the event, none of that happened. As I waded through my own disbelief and discovered the reality of my pregnancy there was no screaming or shouting. I felt as though I was simply stepping from a waiting room into my receiving and experienced both a strange peace and a sense of loss. A small part of me was grieving the end of our wait. I had learned to wait, I had known comfort and the closeness of Christ in my pain. My waiting came to an end with a quiet smile of understanding – this was God's way . . . and God's time!

We're restless, Lord, help us to learn to rest because you rest. May we know you in the waiting times and understand you more in the way you wait. In learning to trust you – and your timing – may we grow more like you.

* * *

Instant expectation versus God's timing

'If you spend yourselves on behalf of the hungry and satisfy the needs of the oppressed, then your light will rise in the darkness, and your night will become like the noonday.

The LORD will guide you always; he will satisfy your needs in a sun-scorched land and will strengthen your frame. You will be like a well-watered garden, like a spring whose waters never fail. Your people will rebuild the ancient ruins and will raise up the age-old foundations; you will be called Repairer of Broken Walls, Restorer of Streets with Dwellings. If you keep your feet from breaking the Sabbath and from doing as you please on my holy day, if you call the Sabbath a delight and the LORD's holy day honourable, and if you honour it by not going your own way and not doing as you please or speaking idle words, then you will find your joy in the LORD, and I will cause you to ride on the heights of the land and to feast on the inheritance of your father Jacob.' The mouth of the LORD has spoken.

(Isaiah 58.10–14)

The Bible is full of wonderful promises such as this – and God still gives promises to his people, yet most are for the future and seldom fulfilled without a time of waiting. Abraham had to wait for his promised son; Israel had to wait for her promised land. Later Israel waited to be rescued from her oppressive rulers, expecting a Messiah who would do just that. I wonder, even without human fault delaying things further, would God have built waiting into the timetable? Without it would we ever have grown big enough to be ready to receive such blessing?

In this passage, Israel has been attempting to hurry God along by intensifying religious observances, including fasting. By contrast he had been waiting for his punishment of the nation to restore their special relationship through an honest response. He wanted a grown-up relationship of trust, faith, hope, love – not manipulative religion.

God designed the Sabbath not as a complicated series of laws almost impossible for human beings to keep, but as a delight – a day when slaves and servants might rest alongside their masters, trusting in God's provision, revelling in time 'wasted' with him. Do we have those Sabbath moments, if not days, in our lives? Moments when we dismiss worry, fret and hurry and allow ourselves to experience joy, to 'ride on the heights', whatever our circumstances? If that sounds selfish, we can only love others in as much as we know we are loved ourselves. Who knows what might flow from time we invest in letting God show his love for us?

But what if the promise God has given you is about spending yourself on behalf of the hungry and satisfying the needs of the oppressed? That sounds urgent – yet even St Paul had to wait before receiving God's go-ahead to take the gospel to the Gentiles – and later waited in various prisons too.

Jan King, retired missionary, writes:

The excitement of it all. Here I was aged sixty, a classics teacher nearing retirement, who had just received a very clear call from God to be a missionary! 'My' verse said, 'I will guide you continually and satisfy your needs in a sun-scorched land.' Africa Inland Mission had accepted me, assigned me to go as a teacher and Kenya was to be the 'sun-scorched land'. Full of excitement, I began my preparations. Then came the devastating phone call. 'Sit down, Jan,' came the voice. I sat. 'They won't have you because you're divorced.'

I hung up and sat in silence, trying to take it in. Questions bombarded me. 'What is God doing?' 'Why, why, why?' I had resigned from my teaching post, I was recently divorced and facing a very uncertain future in which loneliness loomed large. Suddenly I'd been told that church schools in Kenya – and most of Africa – do not agree with divorce in any circumstances. I shouted at God, I cried, I pleaded for some light on the situation – then, at long last, I began to pray.

My school took me back and I resumed my everyday life. A full year later, I met a retired missionary couple from Sudan. As I listened to them and saw their pictures my heart was suddenly warmed. This was it! I knew that this was not just a chance meeting, it was God unfolding his master plan.

I finally set off for Africa, two years older but much wiser. God had known that he still had work to do within me here in the UK, to shape me for his service in Africa. I found myself doing specialist work preparing literacy materials – another of God's mini-miracles. My School Certificate mark for my worst subject, English, had been only 53 per cent. But I've always had a love for words and my classical training proved useful in writing about English grammar. While in Kenya, I visited the school where I might have taught. I was able to thank my all-knowing God for closing that door and opening up a door to southern Sudan, with all its joys and sorrows – and for putting me in the very place where he could use me to further his work in that wonderful but suffering part of his world.

As I write this Jan, now aged seventy-three, is about to return once again to southern Sudan for a month to teach four year-groups of Sudanese pastors and two year-groups of illiterate pastors' wives. What will this English failure be teaching? English, of course!

Looking backwards, Lord, it's easy to see how you work your purposes out far better than any human could have done. Yet, I know that if I'm kept waiting, I grumble. Help us to remember that we wait on you, not you on us. Help us to make the most of your gift of waiting times – to find delight, strength and refreshment for the task ahead by simply 'being' with you rather than busying ourselves to death with always 'doing'. Help us to follow your culture, your ways, your timing. Help us to see from your perspective that what we think of as waste, you can redeem. Help us to wait, and thus to live, well.

God's time and ways: waiting in the wrong place

Now a man came up to Jesus and asked, 'Teacher, what good thing must I do to get eternal life?'

. . . Jesus replied, '. . . If you want to enter life, obey the commandments.'

. . . 'All these I have kept,' the young man said. 'What do I still lack?'

Jesus answered, 'If you want to be perfect, go, sell your possessions and give to the poor, and you will have treasure in heaven. Then come, follow me.'

When the young man heard this, he went away sad, because he had great wealth.

Then Jesus said to his disciples, '. . . it is easier for a camel to go through the eye of a needle than for a rich man to enter the kingdom of God.'

When the disciples heard this, they were greatly astonished and asked, 'Who then can be saved?'

Jesus looked at them and said, 'With man this is impossible, but with God all things are possible.'

(Matthew 19.16–26)

So nearly right and yet so far from the truth – that young man's story is one of the saddest in the Gospels because obeying the best of laws would never bring him the wonderful eternal life he awaited. Only following Jesus wholeheartedly would lead him in that direction. The disciples weren't much better. They had yet to grasp the fundamental importance of faith – that salvation comes from God, it's not something we can earn. How silly, when you come to think of it, to assume that puny human beings could ever earn the right to become immortal, let alone relate to the all-powerful, eternal Father, Son and Holy Spirit.

The Bible contains plenty more examples of people who waited in the wrong place, in the wrong ways, at the wrong time and/or for the wrong thing. Most obviously the Jews waited centuries for a Messiah who would deliver them from the hated Roman occupiers of their land. On one level that wasn't unreasonable – God had delivered them from many enemies in the past, from invasion, even from exile. But this time everything had changed. God was offering them a very different sort of freedom through a sacrificial lamb in the shape of his own Son. Most of them didn't recognize the One they had waited for. I'm not sure I would have done.

It's so easy to be convinced that we're right, when we're not, especially over spiritual matters. The basic mistake is usually a misunderstanding of the ways of God, just as the anecdote below concerns a basic misunderstanding of the ways of rail timetables.

Ann Hallson, a legal secretary living in Surrey, tells how she once waited in vain, because she was waiting in the wrong place, at the wrong time:

> My work-task over for that day, I was allowed to go straight home rather than return to the office, so I made my way to London's Charing Cross Station to catch the train to Caterham. It was the beginning of the rush hour as I strode across the station concourse, confident in the knowledge that I was in the right place. I studied the timetable boards but could see no sign of my train's departure. I wandered around, checked the boards, wandered around again and, with neck craned, checked the boards once more, but still found no departure platform for my train nor heard any announcements.
>
> By now I had been waiting for a considerable time and, concerned that I had forgotten some vital element, began a mental process of elimination. I knew for definite that my train left from Charing Cross; I was standing at Charing Cross – so where was my train?
>
> Then I realized that although Caterham trains left from this station, they did so only at weekends and out of rush hour. Other than that, they left from London Bridge, a couple of stations down the line.
>
> Feeling foolishly weary I travelled to London Bridge where the Caterham train was waiting – and arrived home much later than normal that evening.

From this experience early in my career I learned that I could not always rely on my own judgement to know whether I was in the right place. I would have been wiser – and saved time – had I asked someone for help.

Lord, help us when we wait to check with you that we're waiting for the right thing, in the right way, at the right time and place. Help us bear in mind those words from Isaiah 55.9: 'As the heavens are higher than the earth, so are my ways higher than your ways and my thoughts than your thoughts.' Help us to understand not only about you – for example your commands and what you've done historically – but to learn to understand your ways. Help us as we follow you not to forget that it's all about relating with you – in busy times and in waiting times.

Waiting for . . .

To be filled, to flow and be fulfilled,
To glow and grow and maybe overflow
To thrill and spill and, enthralled, to fall –
No!
Keep me, never let me go!

O Master, who knows me through and through,
Farmer, sow in me seed that grows slow and true to you;
Mother, sew my tattered dress!
Surgeon, sew my wounds!
Healer, disinfect my heart!
Oh, I hurt, when you don't race to do.
But you, I AM, you live to be.

Be then my centre – of gravity, of laughter.
Weight me.

*   *   *

Waiting for . . . *something good*

On tenterhooks

People were bringing little children to Jesus to have him touch
them, but the disciples rebuked them. When Jesus saw this, he
was indignant. He said to them, 'Let the little children come to
me, and do not hinder them, for the kingdom of God belongs
to such as these. I tell you the truth, anyone who will not receive
the kingdom of God like a little child will never enter it.'

And he took the children in his arms, put his hands on them
and blessed them.   (Mark 10.13–16)

In many of the stories and Bible passages in this book we see
how people have to learn to wait. By contrast, I love this one,
where Jesus commands that no one should hinder children in
coming to him. It's true of adults too – we don't have to wait
to come to Jesus. If we adults run to him like children, don't
you find that, at the very least, he will bless us, even if we do
have to wait for whatever it is we want? Of course for young
children, some things won't wait, as Kathy Barnes writes, calling this piece about her own childhood 'On tenterhooks'.

Why does Mummy always say, 'Wait a minute!'? If I'm busy
doing something really important and it's bedtime, I sometimes
say, 'Just a minute . . .' but Mummy says, 'No. Now!' and I have
to go. But if I want her to help, she always says, 'Wait a minute,
I'm on the phone. Wait a minute, I'm reading the paper. Wait
a minute, I'm just going to have a shower.' It's not fair. My teacher told us that a minute isn't very long, although when we all
had to sit still without speaking for a whole minute it seemed
more like half an hour. Mummy's minutes take ages.

I've been sitting by the window since breakfast looking
at the snow. It was already there a bit when I got up. I could
still see the path and the steps, but now it's snowing hard and
everything has disappeared – it's really thick. It's Saturday and
I can't wait to get out there and make a snowman. Mummy
says I've got to put on my coat, hat, gloves and boots but I
don't mind if I get cold. I want to go *now*! 'Please, Mummy,
I know you were having a lie in, but could you hurry up and
finish your coffee? . . . But there won't be any snow later. You
know what happened last time – we waited and waited and
then it rained . . . I promise I won't throw snowballs at you –
honestly. Are you coming? I've got my boots on and . . . Hooray!
Let's go!'

16

I have the feeling that Jesus was as impatient to see and hug the children as they were to meet him – or as Kathy was to play in the snow. Perhaps the Lord's waiting for us, his children, isn't so very unlike us waiting for our own children to return – think of Jesus' story of the prodigal son. Penny Clarke describes waiting for a son's return, not from pigs and prostitutes but from a journey which held some danger:

September – the day has come at last and my son is setting off from Harwich to travel overland, most of the way, down to Kenya – not something recommended in any travel brochures I have seen. But I tell myself he will be with others and hopefully all will be well.

The odd postcard arrives, the odd email, but I know it is not easy to keep in touch. Glad to hear Ethiopia is cool and he is not near the war zone with Eritrea – that's something I suppose. Time is passing now, and he is in Rwanda watching gorillas. Not long now until the end of the journey – not long till he will catch a plane back from Nairobi. Not long – I can hardly wait to see him again.

Am just taking the washing out of the machine at 11.00 a.m. when the phone goes. 'Hi Mum – are you busy?'

'Where are you, where are you?'

'Victoria Station. Can you pick me up at Epsom?'

My heart is beating so fast. I fly upstairs, check the bedroom that has been ready since he left – I know, but just checking. Put some lipstick on – as if he cares! Please don't let the car play up. Park outside the station. Can hear the train come in. Can hardly bear the waiting now and then there he is – hair grown bushy, a beard that was not there in September, carrying the largest skin-covered drum I have ever seen.

I rush up. Fling my arms around him, my eyes are misty. A voice penetrates my senses. 'Hi Mum, I'm back.' The waiting is over and he is safely home. There is so much to catch up on. One more hug. 'Mum, people are looking!'

In Jesus' day children (and women) weren't considered worthy of much attention, and yet, despite being tired, despite having many important things to do, Jesus made himself available to them, welcomed them, rejoiced over them as a parent might at the return of a long-lost son or daughter. Draw near to him now, assured of that welcome – don't hang back, don't wait!

*   *   *

Waiting for . . . *something good while suffering injustice*

Do not fret because of evil men or be envious of those who do
    wrong; for like the grass they will soon wither, like green
    plants they will soon die away.
Trust in the Lord and do good; dwell in the land and enjoy
    safe pasture.
Delight yourself in the Lord and he will give you the desires
    of your heart.
Commit your way to the Lord; trust in him and he will do
    this:
He will make your righteousness shine like the dawn, the
    justice of your cause like the noonday sun.
Be still before the Lord and wait patiently for him; do not fret
    when men succeed in their ways, when they carry out their
    wicked schemes.
Refrain from anger and turn from wrath; do not fret – it leads
    only to evil.
For evil men will be cut off, but those who hope in the Lord
    will inherit the land.

(Psalm 37.1–9)

'Delight yourself in the Lord.' What a lovely thought for a time of waiting – sure beats fretting, anger and envy! I've just heard on the TV news that scientists say happy people live on average nine years longer than unhappy people. If fretting, envy and the harbouring of anger are sin, then those scientists, along with the ancient lyrics of Psalm 37, shine an interesting light on Romans 6.23: 'For the wages of sin is death, but the gift of God is eternal life in Christ Jesus our Lord.'

So, as we wait, why do we often choose fretting, anger and envy over delighting, trusting and doing good? The other day a lorry overturned on the M25. A journey to work which should have taken a colleague of my husband twenty minutes lasted over three hours of stop–start misery involving thousands of motorists. When she explained, my husband was full of sympathy, yet she seemed unfrazzled, even content. 'When I drove past and saw the mess being cleared up I was just so grateful that no other vehicle was involved,' she said, embarking calmly on her tasks of the day.

Sometimes I think it's a bit like a spider's web – especially when we're caught up in some injustice. Those who relax and trust are more likely to be rescued. If we kick and shout – fret – then we'll become further entangled and probably attract the attention of the big, hairy spider, hungry to gobble up the best bits of us.

Jesus identified with all those who suffer injustice – went to the cross innocent, bearing the consequences of all fretting, malice, envy and anger, while waiting, trusting in God, doing only good. Does that take away the shame, the sting when our waiting is for deliverance from injustice? Does that show a way to behave in the web of powerlessness which we feel – the way towards trust in rescue which will come, even if it's after everyone else has given up hope? Maybe that big, bad, hairy spider has been robbed of its power to catch us, unless we choose to be caught.

Brigitte Furze, a nature-loving musician, writes:

In Psalm 37.4 David claims that if we love God, he will give us the desire of our heart. But it does not say when that will happen.

It was an exciting step for us: after renting a lovely flat for a couple of years, my husband and I were moving into our very own property. It was on the top floor of a newly converted Georgian house. I loved the space and light of the freshly decorated rooms, the nooks and crannies created by the sloping ceiling, but most of all I was excited about having a share of the garden. I didn't mind the thought of months of hard work to change the reigning jungle into flowerbeds, a vegetable patch and a play area for our expected first child.

One day, to my surprise, I came home to find my washing line had been taken down and put on our doorstep. When I asked around, the couple who had moved, after us, into the ground-floor flat said they had only bought it because they had sole use of the garden. Showing them our lease didn't change their response – my dream had been stolen, and I was struggling with my anger. But when friends suggested we take our neighbours to court, I didn't feel at ease either. So I asked God, 'How can this be right?'

When next morning I 'happened' to read in my Bible, 'If any one wants to . . . take your tunic, let him have your coat also,' I thought oh-oh-oh! Then I bought a bouquet of flowers for the couple on the ground floor. It didn't stop me from looking down longingly, first when they sifted the earth of the entire garden, and later when they picked their beans. But I had peace.

A few years later we moved again into a flat with a shared garden – this time none of the other parties was interested in gardening, and the landlord said we could do what we wanted out there. That is where our strawberries grew more abundantly than ever since.

Lord, I'm so bad at waiting patiently, especially when even a small injustice is involved. Your way can seem so counter-intuitive. I'm not naturally meek, yet verse 11 of this psalm contains the words Jesus repeated later: 'Blessed are the meek, for they will inherit the earth' (Matthew 5.5). Help me to wait in the way you have shown – and to pray for the millions who suffer years of injustice of an order I've never known.

* * *

Waiting for . . . *an end to injustice*

Be merciful to me, O God, for men hotly pursue me; all day long they press their attack. My slanderers pursue me all day long; many are attacking me in their pride.

When I am afraid, I will trust in you. In God, whose word I praise, in God I trust; I will not be afraid. What can mortal man do to me? All day long they twist my words; they are always plotting to harm me. They conspire, they lurk, they watch my steps, eager to take my life. (Psalm 56.1–6)

The psalmist is waiting – for what? More slander and unjust accusations? A lynching? No – remarkably, in this moment when he's under direct attack, he says, 'In God I trust. What can mortal man do to me?' He affirms, 'I will not be afraid.' The psalm ends with: 'You have delivered me from death and my feet from stumbling, that I may walk before God in the light of life.' He's remembering how God delivered him in the past, trusting him for the present and looking forward to a great life with him in the future. He's doing all the right things, keeping the right attitude. What a spiritual giant! Why can't I be like that?

But hang on a minute, this is David – that great hero of faith who walked closely with God but sometimes did everything wrong – and the Bible is honest enough to admit it. The introduction to this psalm says that it is about the time when the Philistines seized David in Gath. In fact David had fled to Gath of his own accord, after jealous Saul had tried to kill him. His great friend, Saul's son Jonathan, had warned him to leave the country. But David had no safe place to go, no one to go with him and nothing to eat but the consecrated bread from the temple. Considering also that he was still waiting for the fulfilment of God's long-ago promise that he was to be king, this was an emotional and physical low point. David had shown only kindness and love towards Saul and Jonathan and fought for them with great courage but now, hurt, rejected, vulnerable, he didn't know where to turn. In this narrative there is no record that he turned to God. Maybe he wrote Psalm 56 years later, in the rosy glow of hindsight.

At the time, things became worse. For some reason David chose to flee, of all places, to the Philistine king of Gath. Remember that David had killed the giant, Goliath? He came from Gath. The Philistines were prime enemies during that whole period in Israel's history. Yet David realized that his choice of refuge wasn't exactly wise only when the king's servants started singing, 'Saul has slain his thousands, and David his tens of thousands.' At that moment David became 'very much afraid of Achish king of Gath. So he feigned insanity in their presence; and while he was in their hands he acted like a madman, making marks on the doors of the gate and letting saliva run down his beard' (1 Samuel 21.12–13). He doesn't sound quite so much the hero of faith now, does he?

Next he escapes to the cave of Adullam. 'When his brothers and his father's household heard about it, they went down to him there. All those who were in distress or in debt or discontented gathered round him, and he became their leader' (1 Samuel 22.1–2). What a rabble – this wasn't a promising start to the reign of the best king Israel ever had! Or was it? David's descendant, Jesus, also gathered around him those who were distressed or in debt, the outcasts of society, the sinners and the discontented – and as they made him their King, their Lord, his life slowly but surely transformed theirs.

Isn't it comforting that God remains faithful, even when human beings like ourselves and David aren't? The Bible shows us how to react to injustice or pressure, slander or violence – but even if we behave more like spiritual imbeciles than giants, God's grace has the power to redeem. Despite appearances during the waiting period when injustice seems to triumph, his passion that human beings should live in justice and righteousness never dims.

Normally it's worse to see someone you love suffering than to go through it yourself. If David was hurt, how much worse did Jonathan feel about his father's terrible actions which resulted in him having to tell his own best friend to flee for his life? Former GP Amanda Hoskins writes about a time when her son and his young family suffered injustice. Another psalm of David spoke to her at the time – Psalm 37.1–11, the same passage which spoke to Brigitte Furze (see page 20).

I'd been delighted at the way things were working out for our son, Sam. He had married a lovely girl and our second grand-child was on the way. Of course they'd have a bit of a struggle financially supporting themselves and two little ones on what he earned as a psychiatric nurse but he loved his work. They'd moved quite a distance to an area with more affordable housing. They'd even settled in a church where they felt accepted and much loved.

And then – disaster. Sam and three colleagues were suspended from work following allegations of misconduct. Though these had no foundation in truth I saw Sam robbed not only of overtime pay but of any confidence in himself. If the case went against him and the others, their whole future would be in doubt.

As we all waited, everything seemed negative – no information, no dates, no end in sight and nothing anyone could do about it. Sam lost weight and became depressed. He felt so helpless. So did his wife, so did we and the other set of parents. Work offered no support – but his church did. Their care was one of the few bright spots. Even so, I found myself asking God, 'Why?' It seemed so unjust. Sam had really thrown himself into his work and cared so much for the patients he served. How could envious co-workers wreck good young lives? Surely someone should be doing something about this?

As I prayed, Psalm 37 caught my eye. It describes a similar situation but says: 'Be still before the LORD and wait patiently for him; do not fret when men succeed in their ways, when they carry out their wicked schemes. Refrain from anger and turn from wrath; do not fret – it leads only to evil. For evil men will be cut off, but those who hope in the LORD will inherit the land.' Was God making a promise? My heart lifted. I believed he was.

After a long wait, Sam and the others were fully exonerated and returned to work. Even better, now he, his wife and two children have moved to live closer to us again and Sam is enjoying a new start in his career with a different health authority.

Pray for those who suffer injustice, or who watch loved ones doing so. Pray especially for those who flee in the wrong direction, as David did. Pray that God will speak to them in their pain and fear, in their bitter sense of rejection – and restore their faith, their hope and their love, those three things which he promised will endure.

*   *   *

Waiting for . . . *social justice*

How long will the wicked, O LORD, how long will the wicked be jubilant? They pour out arrogant words; all the evildoers are full of boasting. They crush your people, O LORD; they oppress your inheritance. They slay the widow and the alien; they murder the fatherless. They say, 'The LORD does not see; the God of Jacob pays no heed.' . . . Who will rise up for me against the wicked? Who will take a stand for me against evildoers?

Unless the LORD had given me help, I would soon have dwelt in the silence of death. When I said, 'My foot is slipping,' your love, O LORD, supported me. When anxiety was great within me, your consolation brought joy to my soul.

(Psalm 94.3–7, 16–19)

The waiting psalmist asks God, 'How long?' as though God's to blame. Don't we often do something similar? Tsunami, 9/11, famine in Africa, conflict between nations, unfair trade and exploitation, slavery, pollution, violence, racism, climate change . . . Is God to blame or could we do something about all of these things? OK, maybe we couldn't have stopped the tsunami but are horrendously slow to put early-warning systems in place which would save so many lives.

When faced with large-scale human suffering and social injustice, plenty of people think that God doesn't see, or care, that he's dead or fallen asleep. But the psalm goes on to say, 'Take heed, you senseless ones among the people; you fools, when will you become wise? Does he who implanted the ear not hear? Does he who formed the eye not see?' (Psalm 94.8–9). And then he asks who will work with him to put things right. How different the world would be if we did that: if each one of us heeded the Bible's oft-repeated cry for social justice – to care for those who are marginalized or oppressed.

25

But surely we can't take all that on, can we? Who are we to take a stand against all the evils in this world? There again, the psalm has an answer. God's love isn't there merely so that we can feel nice and warm and comfortable. The psalmist said it did support him though, as he bit off considerably more than he thought he could chew in response to the Lord's call to become involved.

One person who did choose to get involved is Pat Price-Tomes, retired from running a project for a voluntary organization. A mother of six and grandmother, Pat spent two stints of three months each in Palestine with an ecumenical, multinational peace organization. Their teams' tasks are to monitor and communicate the situation and to accompany individuals who need support. That involves the teams in a good deal of waiting, but for the local people it is far worse. Pat writes of one experience in 2004:

We were on our way from Nablus, one of the biggest cities in the Occupied Palestinian Territories, to visit Jenin and its infamous refugee camp.

Waiting is endemic to journeys in Palestine; our first experience of Shave Shomron checkpoint, to the north of Nablus, was the longest of my time in the West Bank.

The crowd was heaving and pressing against the barrier, the queues (men one side, women the other) were long, and the fierce summer sun bore down on the young men herded like sheep in the concrete 'pen', waiting for their IDs to be checked. Disgruntled, some claimed to have been there for three hours or more.

None of the women around us in the crowd spoke English, though clearly they wanted to tell us their stories. Many were trying to manage and protect fractious children. As we drew closer to the barrier, any residual notion of queuing faded. We were going to have to push and shove like the rest.

A little lady was inching forward ahead of us, moving her shopping bags (all ten of them) in relays. We soon realized that she wasn't fully alert – she was being bypassed by all and sundry. She would never get through without help.

So we formed a human barrier around her, the three of us, edging her gently in the right direction and ruthlessly holding back the heaving crowd.

How no one became trapped in the recently installed turnstile I will never know (limbs have been broken since). Eventually we manoeuvred our little lady and all her bags safely into it and out on the other side.

Finally we too were through, and arrived at the counter; the Israeli soldier who took our passports for checking told us there had been a suicide bombing in Beer Sheva (way south in Israel), which demanded extra security at all checkpoints – reminding us that fear on both sides constantly raises the temperature of the conflict.

We moved aside to wait with the young men in the 'pen'. But no, we were not allowed to wait there, because 'they are in check'. 'So are we,' we responded, fruitlessly. It appears that foreigners rank more highly than local Palestinians and must not be allowed to contaminate themselves.

We thought it wise not to raise the obvious question as to why it took less time to check our passports than to carry out the more routine checking of local IDs; we were able to continue on our journey about an hour and a half after arriving, leaving behind an angry, frustrated crowd.

For us, a small insight and a story to tell; for Palestinians a daily assault on their dignity and ability to lead a normal life with all the opportunities which we take for granted. A reminder that for some in the world, waiting is a way of life on which survival depends; and that those involved in the conflict in Israel–Palestine face a long wait for a just peace.

Information on what you might do in response is available from the Ecumenical Accompaniment Programme in Palestine and Israel

(EAPPI) <quaker.org.uk/eappi> <www.machsomwatch.org/en> will
tell you more about the checkpoints <www.btselem.org> is a good
site for wider information.

Ask God if he's waiting for you to do something for a few
of the many millions in this world who are waiting for social
justice or for alleviation of terrible suffering which they cannot
escape. Does he want you to pray, give or raise money, write
letters, go . . . or what?

*   *   *

Waiting for . . . *recovery from damage*

Woe to him who quarrels with his Maker, to him who is but a
potsherd among the potsherds on the ground. Does the clay
say to the potter, 'What are you making?' Does your work say,
'He has no hands'?

Woe to him who says to his father, 'What have you begot-
ten?' or to his mother, 'What have you brought to birth?'

This is what the LORD says – the Holy One of Israel, and its
Maker: Concerning things to come, do you question me about
my children, or give me orders about the work of my hands?

(Isaiah 45.9–11)

When one of his toys broke, my small son used to put it in
'Daddy's mending cupboard', utterly confident that it would
emerge after a few days as good as new. Normally it did, but
we opened the car door in Wales once and he questioned
whether all was well with a nearby sheep whose legs stuck stiffly
upwards. When we told him that it was dead, he said, 'Poor
sheep!' then brightened. 'Daddy mend it, de dead sheep!' That
Daddy couldn't mend the dead sheep had nothing to do with
our being hundreds of miles from the mending cupboard. Our
son lost a tiny bit of his innocent trust that day.

What about God, who, with or without cupboards, can mend dead things, sick people, broken lives? Did we believe that once but now we're not so sure? When we're damaged and broken, waiting on our own in the dark for some kind of help to come, do we lose our trust in ourselves, in others, in God? Do we assume that he's lost faith in us – start to think that we're fatally flawed, beyond redemption? That seems to be the diagnosis in Isaiah's prophecy. But God can mend even broken fragments of pot, as Lindsay Duncombe, a builder's administrator, writes:

I had a breakdown. My mind was shattered into thousands of tiny pieces. Like a vase, dropped from a height, I hit the floor and the tiny fragments scattered in all directions. Some very special people stood by me and prevented those pieces from scattering too far ever to collect again but as a person I felt so broken. I had no idea of how to rebuild my life again, or even if I wanted to.

I functioned on the most basic level. My mind was so damaged I couldn't read more than a paragraph at a time. At the same time everything became deeply meaningful and my faith was crucial to me. I found Isaiah 30.15 particularly helpful: 'This is what the Sovereign Lord, the Holy One of Israel, says: "In repentance and rest is your salvation, in quietness and trust is your strength."'

I used to sit for hours in the garden and I spent time just being. After years using Herculean strength to deal with one trauma after another, both mind and body were exhausted. Walking across the room would be as much as I could manage. I moved from chair to chair, spending most of my time asleep.

My adrenaline pump had broken, and I was petrified of people. When I finally ventured out of the house, it was on the arm of my father who could keep me safe from the harm I perceived from everyone and anyone. My children would have to take my hands and lead me gently down the high street, talking to me constantly to reassure me.

Yes, there was waiting – years of waiting, but I didn't know what for. I really wanted to wait until I died, because I couldn't see how I could ever recover. But recover, slowly, slowly, inch by painful inch, I did.

I could never look up and catch a glimpse of the journey I would have to make to recovery, because whenever I did that I would stumble and fall, only to be picked up again gently by those who loved and cared for me, brushed down and led on yet again.

When I started that journey, I had no idea of what shape I would be when I finished, what I would look like, what my personality would be like – I felt the mould had been broken and there was nothing left.

My marriage was over, and I had to find a new home for myself and the children. I knew that there was a possibility of having a bungalow built behind our house, and there followed months of agonizing uncertainty, waiting for the planning permission to be passed. The worst thing for me was feeling so out of control of what could happen – I knew that if permission wasn't passed I wouldn't be able to afford to live in that area and dreaded the thought of having to move away from everything that was so familiar to me. I would phone the council regularly for news – any setback plunged me into despair and sent me scuttling back to the architect for reassurance.

I felt I couldn't move on from my old life until I was able to move into my new home. While waiting I was trapped, like a butterfly waiting to emerge and longing to stretch out its wings and to feel the sun on them after so long in darkness. My new walls would keep me safe, and allow me to spread those wings without getting trampled on again.

By the time we could make a start, I was getting stronger. In having my own home built, I was rebuilding my life too, and as the walls went up and the roof went on, so my healing continued.

Finally on Christmas Eve 2004, I opened the door and walked in. I was home.

Especially if you are waiting for recovery from damage, you might like to meditate on these verses:

> We are the clay, you are the potter; we are all the work of your hand. (Isaiah 64.8)

> The Spirit of the Sovereign LORD is on me, because the LORD has anointed me to preach good news to the poor. He has sent me to bind up the broken-hearted, to proclaim freedom for the captives and release from darkness for the prisoners . . . They will rebuild the ancient ruins and restore the places long devastated; they will renew the ruined cities that have been devastated for generations. (Isaiah 61.1, 4)

* * *

Waiting for . . . *God-given dreams and visions to be fulfilled*

> I will stand at my watch and station myself on the ramparts; I will look to see what he will say to me, and what answer I am to give to this complaint. Then the LORD replied: 'Write down the revelation and make it plain on tablets so that a herald may run with it. For the revelation awaits an appointed time; it speaks of the end and will not prove false. Though it linger, wait for it; it will certainly come and will not delay.'
> (Habakkuk 2.1–3)

'It will not delay.' Yet strangely, according to the words God spoke to his prophet Habakkuk, it may well 'linger'. Which seems horribly like delay when you're waiting for something important. 'No madam, your parcel hasn't been delayed, it's just . . . lingering somewhere' isn't too convincing.

Maybe what's in the parcel has yet to be made. Maybe it can't be made, or grown, at this season of the year. I suspect people in Habakkuk's day were more used to this kind of waiting than we are, when strawberries are air-freighted from the other side of the world to our supermarket shelves in winter and factories manufacture goods at speeds unimaginable to the craftsmen of biblical times.

Goods that we've ordered are one thing. There should be some paper or electronic trail, maybe even of where the parcel was last seen. God-given dreams, promises and visions, however 'plain' and obvious they appeared at first, are something else. As we wait and watch faithfully for them, time goes by and we (I, anyway) start to doubt. Was this really God, or merely my fervent-but-foolish wish?

I met Tricia Phillips on a Mediterranean holiday. She had a good job as a public sector executive, a good church, loved God and was great company. But she was growing no younger – and hadn't God promised her a husband? A few years later, on another Mediterranean holiday, I spotted Tricia again – this time with her new and delightful husband, Graham. I asked her to write something for this book. She's entitled it:

Waiting for a husband . . . or parcel!

In May 1991 I was given a very clear promise from God, in answer to my broken-hearted prayer for a husband. The thing I most deeply desired God had prepared for me, and this was con-firmed by a picture of a parcel, a gift for me, which had been delayed in the post. And so began a period of waiting for my 'parcel' to arrive. During that time, I adopted various strat-egies. Not knowing how long the wait might be, I started with a lot of enthusiasm!

I began in a state of expectancy and anticipation, looking at every man in church, in the street, wondering – could it be him? Will I meet him today? (Absolutely exhausting emotionally.) I then tried bringing in reinforcements. I signed up twenty Christian friends to pray for my future husband, rationalizing that 'he' must exist so praying for 'him' might speed 'him' to me. I then tried helping God out by going on Christian holidays and to Christian singles events so it would be easier for God to cause us to meet – ridiculous! I also worked hard at putting myself right with God, making sure there were no blockages in me that might be hindering the delivery of my 'parcel'!

Eventually, I gave up striving and just got on with my life. In 1996 I took on a new and challenging job which, together with home, family and church commitments, demanded all my time and emotional energy. Thoughts of a husband were relegated to the back-burner. So imagine my shock when one day my 'parcel' turned up! A Christian colleague walked into my office one lunchtime and asked me out. I was so not expecting it, that it took a week of nagging from God even to say yes to a first date. Finally God convinced me and eighteen months later we were married.

So what did I learn during those eleven years and seven months of waiting?

- If God promises something, it will happen, but you can't hurry it up by anything you do.
- If God has prepared something for you, you won't have to struggle and search to find it. Similarly, God won't let you miss it. He doesn't play games with us.
- If we wait for God, for his timing and his answer, we will not be disappointed.
- His way is perfect.

Single friends still ask me what I 'did' that finally got my prayer answered. The answer is probably – nothing! God is not a fruit

machine on which I finally pressed the 'right button'. Probably
I gave up being desperate and just got on with my life, until
one day, as Scripture says, 'the time had fully come' and so it
happened, as God promised it would.

Lord, when you give a definite promise, or confirm that one of
our most potent dreams will come to pass, it's really hard when
nothing appears to happen. Help us neither to lose sight of your
promise nor to obsess about it. That's a big ask, Lord – we're
only human! And we don't see everything clearly – for example
that we're maturing in the process or that you want us to complete something now that we won't be able to do then. Be with
us in the waiting. Help us to enjoy all the good things that life
offers in the meanwhile. Help us to listen to you, day by day,
in the little things – and then help us do what you say.

* * *

Waiting for . . . good to come while in a difficult place

No king is saved by the size of his army; no warrior escapes by
his great strength. A horse is a vain hope for deliverance;
despite all its great strength it cannot save. But the eyes of the
LORD are on those who fear him, on those whose hope is in his
unfailing love, to deliver them from death and keep them alive
in famine. We wait in hope for the LORD; he is our help and
our shield. In him our hearts rejoice, for we trust in his holy
name. May your unfailing love rest upon us, O LORD, even as
we put our hope in you.   (Psalm 33.16–22)

Armies at war have a poor record of saving people from death
and keeping them alive in famine since war often creates more
problems than it solves. No horse, or nuclear arsenal, is going

to save us from our enemies – only God can do it. That's what this passage is saying but I'm afraid the evidence is that God doesn't always deliver those who love and fear him from death, nor keep them alive in famine – though many are the stories of his doing so, in his own good time, which is often the final minute of the eleventh hour.

So, when our backs are against the wall, are we going to 'jump the gun' and lash out, fighting hard? If we take that way of defeating evil, we're in danger of becoming evil ourselves – that's quite clear from history. Or are we going to put our hope and trust in God's unfailing love which shields us from the psychological damage that fear, hatred and bitterness bring, so that we really can rejoice in him as we wait for rescue? That could be a better strategy, even if we do die.

I'm not sure I'm strong enough to be a pacifist in times of war – and it's probably academic since I'm not of an age to fight. But what about more ordinary situations, where we feel so stuck that we're desperate for something to change? Helene Elston writes:

I'm now retired but for many years I worked as a secretary/PA in a boarding school in southern Ireland. It was a wonderful job, demanding but fulfilling, and exactly right for me. I enjoyed dealing with parents, pupils and staff, and worked in a beautiful Georgian building overlooking green lawns and a fine Victorian chapel.

However, before I began work there I had gone through a period of intense and anguished waiting. I was working in an actuarial practice and, while my boss was kind and friendly, he was frequently out of the office and I was left to type reports on my own in a dismal basement room, which still had bars on the windows from its days as a kitchen!

I prayed so much for release from a job which I realized was not right for me; I even consulted a careers psychologist, who confirmed that I was definitely a square peg in a round hole and needed to change direction. I searched the newspaper ads, signed on with an agency in Dublin, but nothing came up, and I grew more and more frustrated and unhappy.

One afternoon I went to the bank to collect cash for the office. It was a sunny day and I prayed earnestly as I walked. Suddenly in my mind's eye I saw a picture of a bird struggling in the hands of God: the harder it beat its wings the tighter the hands held it, and I understood that to be released it must become still and quiet in his hands.

The message was clear: stop struggling and fretting behind the 'bars' of my office and all would be well. At about this time I also had a vivid dream of a large and tree-filled park. I was walking up a long, steep drive leading to a big house in the distance. Children were running about on the grass slopes.

A few weeks later I rang the agency and this time (almost as an afterthought) they wondered if I would be interested in a job in a boarding school . . .

Months later I realized that it was set in countryside very similar to the place in my dream. It had all been worth waiting for.

Lord, I love that image of a bird, learning to rest still in your hand. Help all of us who struggle and panic to know that, while we wait for something good, you *are* good. Your very nature is love and you whisper, even as we fret, 'The fruit of righteousness will be peace; the effect of righteousness will be quietness and confidence for ever' (Isaiah 32.17).

* * *

Waiting for . . . *God's timing and purposes*

Be dressed ready for service and keep your lamps burning, like men waiting for their master to return from a wedding

banquet, so that when he comes and knocks they can immediately open the door for him. It will be good for those servants
whose master finds them watching when he comes. I tell you
the truth, he will dress himself to serve, will have them recline
at the table and will come and wait on them.

(Luke 12.35–36)

Think story – think 'shape-shifters'. Cinderella, Mrs Doubtfire,
Jekyll and Hyde, werewolves and all those characters in computer
games that transform at the click of a button. All these change
shape quickly, though Cinders has to wait a while before Fairy
Godmother shows up to wave her wand. Transforming the likes
of the Ugly Duckling into a swan, Sméagol into Gollum and
Strider the Ranger into King Aragorn takes longer. That is more
realistic – even Saul's quick change on the Damascus Road pre-
ceded years of waiting and learning before his ministry became
clear. Then, in a few short years as Paul, he spread Christianity
around much of his known world. Simon changed in jerks –
two steps forward, one back – causing himself no end of frustration before he became the steadier Peter-rock on whom Jesus
built his Church. Perhaps shape-shifters appear as archetypes
in many of the best stories because they appear all the time in
'his story'.

In Jesus' parable the servants' job was to wait on their
master – and their lives must have seemed monotonous when
he was absent for any length of time. Those who remained
alert, who stood ready and waiting for their master, ended up
changing shape in a way which must have blown the minds of
Jesus' hearers. On his return the master waited on *them*; they
reclined like honoured guests at his table. That was a quick turn
of events – but wasn't it something in the period of waiting,
specifically their attitude in it, that changed those servants?
During that apparently empty time they learned to set their

hearts on him and on his kingdom, rather than worrying and striving to acquire possessions or honour for themselves. They learned obedience – to be trustworthy, even when no one was looking.

When we're waiting it often appears as if little is happening. We've no proof that it ever will, and little idea of how things would be different if it did. Of course the big story's ending is written in the Bible – the faithful poor will become rich, the weak strong and so on; 1 Corinthians 15.51–52 says, 'We will all be changed – in a flash, in the twinkling of an eye, at the last trumpet.' But what about here and now, when we're frustrated and have no idea of what shape we're supposed to become? Hard though we find it, he's the Master and we're the servants; he's the potter and we're the clay. When God's doing it, our shape-shifting happens according to his way and his timing.

Yvonne Done knew she was at a crossroads in her life. Something needed to change for this one-time teacher whose grown offspring were on the point of leaving home. In her words:

> I arrived at Chris's writing holiday full of expectation and my laptop full of a children's novel. By contrast my husband couldn't see why he had to come along, after all he didn't put pen to paper unless it was absolutely necessary. The result was, we argued most of the way there, all 150 miles.
>
> I have always enjoyed writing, but as I sat in our allocated room, on the edge of my bed, with workshop timetable in one hand and a tissue in the other, writing was the last thing on my mind.
>
> Once we both got involved with the writing warm-up exercises, all the arguments were forgotten and later on in the week Liz, Chris's co-worker, told me about the new era in her life. She described the image of a child's toy that teaches children about shape, by fitting a square or a circle into the correct holes.

'We are like one of those shapes,' she explained. 'Except sometimes God remoulds us so that we can serve a different purpose.'

I realized why Rob and I were in such turmoil; we were clinging on to our old shapes. However, in the peaceful atmosphere of Ashburnham, Rob's form began to take on a new outline: my husband was up at the front performing a poem! When everyone saw my reaction of utter astonishment, they began to laugh. Then I was laughing. I still smile when I think of it today.

Unfortunately, holidays bring a freedom that doesn't always last. Despite this, Rob and I know that it was a foretaste of how we could be, and we are waiting to see where our new forms will lead us, as we let go of the things that prevent our transformation, knowing that with him 'nothing is impossible' (Luke 1.37).

Thank you, Lord, for your transforming power. Help us to trust, during times when nothing seems to be happening, that you know what you are doing, that your purposes are good. Help us to wait on, and wait for you, in a good way.

* * *

Waiting for . . . *something bad*

Waiting *for* . . . something we fear

'Teacher, I brought you my son, who is possessed by a spirit that has robbed him of speech. Whenever it seizes him, it throws him to the ground. He foams at the mouth, gnashes his teeth and becomes rigid. I asked your disciples to drive out the spirit, but they could not.'

'O unbelieving generation,' Jesus replied, 'how long shall I stay with you? How long shall I put up with you? Bring the boy to me.'

So they brought him. When the spirit saw Jesus, it immediately threw the boy into a convulsion. He fell to the ground and rolled around, foaming at the mouth.

Jesus asked the boy's father, 'How long has he been like this?'

'From childhood,' he answered. 'It has often thrown him into fire or water to kill him. But if you can do anything, take pity on us and help us.'

' "If you can"?' said Jesus. 'Everything is possible for him who believes.'

Immediately the boy's father exclaimed, 'I do believe; help me overcome my unbelief!' (Mark 9.17–24)

Exam, operation, pain, loss – we've all waited for something we fear. As I'm writing, people in various parts of England wait helplessly as flood-waters rise. Mediterranean villagers wait as forest fires approach, wondering whether to stay and fight the flames to save their houses or to save their lives and flee. Other people wait under threat of famine, drought, war, terrorist attack . . .

I wonder what it feels like, waiting for a child to have another epileptic fit, or for some disease currently in remission to return. How is it to have a son with schizophrenia, or daughter with a personality disorder, complete with unpredictable behaviour? However positive you try to be it must be so hard not to tense up, waiting for another frightening episode and all the consequences that will bring. What about waiting for a spouse with Alzheimer's to deteriorate until you yourself are stretched beyond your limit? What if you are affected in one of these ways yourself?

It's great that Jesus healed the boy in this story but I do feel sorry for his parents, as for all in this kind of situation. Jesus appears harsh and impatient. Does he mean that, had they prayed or had more faith, bingo, the problem would have been solved? Granted, sometimes miracles happen but more often they don't, despite prayer, despite faith. Jesus was rather better at miracles than we are; we all know of people who never became whole this side of heaven.

These days, medical intervention or drugs might help but, even if available, they don't always work miracles either. Sometimes people have to cope for years with chronic illness which can only deteriorate. I don't believe Jesus grows impatient with those people, I don't believe he castigates them. He's far too compassionate and wants us to be compassionate too – to come alongside people in their fear and anguish, in their separation from 'normal' society, rather than keeping our distance in order to pretend that all's well in God's world.

Stephen Fry had the courage to make a TV documentary about a condition which affects him – 'bipolar' or 'manic' depression. The trailer showed him quietly reading a book while a 'voice off ' commented that he never knew when this thing would strike – the manic phase in which he might do something stupid or illegal, or the depressed phase when suicide becomes a real risk.

Many famous writers and artists, past and present, have suffered from this condition – a mild manic episode can unleash intense creativity. Some honest souls have written movingly about it during my writing holidays and classes. Rosie Berry from Hertfordshire is one of them. She asks:

> How are you labelled? A hoodie, an OAP, 'not in my back yard'? How does 'manic depressive' strike you? With fear or curiosity? Have you ever found yourself washed up in a psychiatric unit? Strange faces examining your strangeness? Drugs reducing your world to a minute, engulfing fear? What boundary have you crossed? Have you humiliated yourself, hurt your best friend? How long will you be kept in synthetic silence?
>
> I too have walked those corridors, called on you – where are you Lord? Have you retreated to the office, where few

dare knock? Interminable cups of tea from a trolley predating the NHS – at least the tea lady, sorry, catering operative, gives me a smile with the unwanted sugar.

Here I try not to lose my name – Rosemary is a bad word for a bad girl – call me Rosie or Rose – you seem like a friend. Lord, I need a friend right now – don't distance yourself with knowing smiles. Safe? Where can I be safe among unknown faces? How do I tell who's staff – why won't you wear your badges? Help me! I'm falling – catch my soul before I lose it.

Lord, have mercy on me.

Pray for yourself or someone you know with real reason to fear as they wait.

* * *

Waiting for . . . illness to take its course

Like a slave longing for the evening shadows, or a hired man waiting eagerly for his wages, so I have been allotted months of futility, and nights of misery have been assigned to me. When I lie down I think, 'How long before I get up?' The night drags on, and I toss till dawn. My body is clothed with worms and scabs, my skin is broken and festering.   (Job 7.2–5)

Sometimes treatments for diseases such as cancer seem worse than the condition, worse than death itself. They might or might not work. To wait for the next treatment and the next, with all the suffering they bring, takes enorm-ous courage. While waiting in such circumstances days seem months, nights interminable. Job wishes he could die, rather than endure such long-drawn-out agony – both physical and emotional (his family have all perished). He tells it like it is and his words remain relevant to many who are seriously ill today.

Meanwhile, where is God? He doesn't put in much by way of appearance from here until nearly the end of the book when he speaks to Job, who replies, 'I know that you can do all things; no plan of yours can be thwarted . . . My ears had heard of you but now my eyes have seen you. Therefore I despise myself and repent in dust and ashes' (Job 42.2, 5–6).

So, in a situation where we are waiting in agony for something even more dire, should we be honest and tell it like it is? Or pretend that God has it sorted and there's nothing to worry about? Job's 'friends' castigate him throughout the book for railing about his situation, yet at the end, 'After the LORD had said these things to Job, he said to Eliphaz the Temanite, "I am angry with you and your two friends, because you have not spoken of me what is right, as my servant Job has"' (Job 42.7).

Our faith is about relationship, and no relationship thrives on denial. God is big enough to take anything we can throw at him, so long as we keep talking – and stop to listen sometimes.

When she heard of a dear friend's diagnosis, head teacher Ann Watts thought back to her own very recent journey through cancer and wrote in her diary,

> Yesterday we heard the news that a very old family friend had been diagnosed with bowel cancer. She was given the news the day before her birthday and is still in the state of shock. She is now waiting for a scan and is very worried about what it might show. I can empathize with her, but not take away the fear. It is such a sharp reminder of how I felt. On a good day, my fears of last year seem so far away, but at the time were very real. The waiting is one of the hardest things to bear.

Ann wrote this prayer-poem for her friend, who sadly died a few months later. Maybe you could use it on your own behalf – or to identify with and intercede for someone you know and love.

Waiting

Yesterday my doctor said,
'You have cancer.'
Three short words, and
somehow,
life cannot be the same.

What do they mean?
Is it a sentence?

How ill am I?
Will I get better?
A thousand questions rush through my mind.

But I do not know any of the answers.

I have to wait,
wait for more tests,
a scan
and more consultations.

Oh God, give me the patience,
the patience to wait for those dates to arrive.

And then
what will the results be?
What will it all mean?
What do I tell my friends?
What do I tell my family
and my children?

Oh God, give me the strength,
the strength to cope with the outcome.

There is no knowing today
what that outcome will be.

Oh God, take away my fear,
give me the courage to face the truth.

And when the tests are over,
the treatment starts.
It may mean an operation,
maybe chemotherapy.
Whatever it is,
it will not be easy.

Oh God, give me the courage to deal with the pain.
Give me patience as I wait,
as I learn to trust
that your love will take me through.

*   *   *

Waiting for . . . *the unknown*

Waiting *for* . . . what might happen?

The boat was already a considerable distance from land,
buffeted by the waves because the wind was against it. During
the fourth watch of the night Jesus went out to them, walking
on the lake. When the disciples saw him walking on the lake,
they were terrified. 'It's a ghost,' they said, and cried out in
fear.

But Jesus immediately said to them: 'Take courage! It is I.
Don't be afraid.'

'Lord, if it's you,' Peter replied, 'tell me to come to you on
the water.'

'Come,' he said. Then Peter got down out of the boat,
walked on the water and came towards Jesus.

But when he saw the wind, he was afraid and, beginning to
sink, cried out, 'Lord, save me!'

> Immediately Jesus reached out his hand and caught him. 'You of little faith,' he said, 'why did you doubt?'
> And when they climbed into the boat, the wind died down.
> (Matthew 14.24–32)

This storm is blowing up out of nowhere. How bad is it going to be? Much worse and we could sink, overturn, be smashed to pieces. What on earth is that . . . that thing, coming towards us? Why is it pretending to be our rabbi? What's going on? People can't walk on water! Oh no, why does Peter have to be so stupid, jumping overboard? He'll drown, just you wait and see!

Can't you hear the music which would be playing if this scene were filmed? It would have to be spooky and crashing all at the same time, portraying fear of the known – the storm – and of the unknown as the disciples waited, helpless and scared witless, to see what would happen next.

I bet those disciples, when they left their nets to follow Jesus, to wait on him, didn't bargain for this kind of thing. They followed him out of familiar territory into the unknown. They spent their lives with him, waiting on his every word, his every move but they didn't 'get it', however much he said or did. They didn't expect him to die, or to rise again. Even after receiving the Holy Spirit, Peter didn't expect to go to the Gentiles.

What about us, when waiting on God takes us towards unknown, dangerous places? We have to let go, to trust him, just as we have to let go of the side of the pool, trusting the water to support us if we're going to swim. But . . . *walking* on water? And what if our waiting and trusting isn't resolved as quickly as Peter's stumble over the waves on a stormy lake? Or involves trusting the Lord for someone else?

Pam Annison, a school-teacher from Herts, wrote this.

When my daughter was twelve she dropped a bombshell. I was delighted that she made a commitment to Jesus when only seven and I told God that I gave her to him like a good believer should. But now . . . did I really mean it?

'Mum, God says I'm going abroad to work for him.'

I was dutifully encouraging but my stomach churned. My two children were all I had. My husband had left when they were small. Although God promised he would be their father, life was financially and emotionally tough. Abroad meant away . . . away from me.

From that summer she began to make choices she believed God was asking of her: school options, how and what to pray, where to spend her hard-earned money, which university, which courses.

I travelled the road with her, praying, talking, keeping quiet, encouraging her to do things that would separate us – so hard, yet I sensed the mother–daughter bond growing stronger and hoped she felt the same. Many times I went to God in tears.

All he said was, 'Didn't you give her to me?'

'Yes, Lord.'

'Well, let go and let me get on with it.'

'But it hurts, Lord.'

'It will hurt a lot less if you stop pulling.'

As we waited for answers, God took us to the edge of our faith. Sometimes the answer would come at the fifty-ninth second of the fifty-ninth minute of the eleventh hour. For example, when her A-level results got mixed up on the day of my cousin's funeral it seemed my daughter's place at the LSE had gone. Her teacher spent hours phoning, organizing and explaining as we sat on tenterhooks, seventy miles away. By afternoon all was OK – but no more of that, please Lord.

Seemingly insurmountable obstacles kept coming but, as we did all we could, waited and prayed, they disappeared just in time. It was exhausting – and didn't stop as she began her first job. We learned a lot about waiting and walking over the storm like Peter. We learned not to interpret God's words but to wait and see exactly how he would do it, as well as when.

And now? At thirty she networks across Europe and America, improving everyday lives of everyday people through her work and expertise. She meets similar practitioners abroad and has been given the 'faith brief' within her work even though her company is not Christian-based. I see her at least twice a month. She lives quite near.

She still meets obstacles; she still has to wait to see her efforts fulfilled. But now she has learned more about waiting and persevering. We are still learning.

Pray especially for those whose waiting involves letting those they love follow Jesus into the unknown.

*   *   *

Waiting for . . . threat – or opportunity for grace and kindness?

In the days when the judges ruled, there was a famine in the land, and a man from Bethlehem in Judah, together with his wife and two sons, went to live for a while in the country of Moab . . . Now Elimelech, Naomi's husband, died . . . her two sons . . . married Moabite women, one named Orpah and the other Ruth. After they had lived there about ten years, both [sons] also died, and Naomi was left without her two sons and her husband. When she heard in Moab that the LORD had come to the aid of his people by providing food for them, Naomi and her daughters-in-law prepared to return home from there . . . and set out on the road that would take them back to the land of Judah.   (Ruth 1.1–7)

So many 'unknowns' face the characters in the book of Ruth. Of course we know that the story ends happily but its dramatic power lies in how vulnerable these people were, especially the women, who knew nothing of what the future held. In the famine they didn't know where their next meal was coming from, nor how they would be received in the foreign country of Moab. The same applied back in Judah – Naomi had been gone a long time, while Ruth was an 'alien'. These two waited on the edge of an uncertain future while poleaxed by grief – aware that their own emotions could catch them off balance at any moment.

In those days, with no males to support her, Naomi would have had no option of living out her days in Moab. Normally daughters-in-law returned to their own families, which is what Orpah did. Ruth chose to follow her mother-in-law along a road which might have been known to Naomi physically but for Ruth led to a new people, a new God, a new life and, eventually, a new marriage. Such was her commitment to Naomi that Ruth travelled 'blind', one step at a time.

Margaret Legg has been coming to one of my creative writing groups for several years now and her life story reminds me of the story of Naomi and Ruth. After Margaret's Canadian husband died she returned to England and lived with her mother, in one room, with her three young children. For years it must have been such a struggle and yet, unlike Naomi, she didn't become bitter. Instead she is always telling us about the good things. In this piece which she wrote in the group, we were all moved by the way she caught hold of the one ray of light, the one positive kindness and even now continues to turn it outwards towards others. So that you know the end of the story, as with Ruth, later Margaret met and married another good man.

Over the years from as far back as I can remember New Year's Eve was a fun time.

'What's your New Year's Eve resolution?' my friends used to ask me. We all had a giggle about it. Then we had a chance to wish for all sorts of silly things, such as 'blowing the biggest bubble' while chewing bubble gum.

As we matured, no more acting like little children, we had more grown-up resolutions, especially after World War II started. But there is one New Year's Eve I will never forget, when I found out in a strange sort of way that there really is someone up there on high who hears us and who communicates with others.

It was snowing hard – not unusual for Canada. I'd served as a Wren in the war and, like many British girls, married a Canadian soldier. After the war we'd settled in a little village in Cape Breton Island, Nova Scotia – not so very different from England. I was so happy there and our family grew. We had two children, with a third on the way, but sadly my husband wasn't well. Injuries from the war continued to trouble him and that snowy New Year's Eve he was in hospital, recovering from an operation. Just before midnight I was alone in the house with the children, all of us asleep, when a loud knocking at the door woke me. Looking out, I heard singing and the ringing of bells. I could see a big sleigh being pulled along by neighbours and by some folk I didn't recognize – they must have lived farther away.

'Happy New Year!' they called.

I ran downstairs, so surprised that I spluttered, 'But it's not midnight yet!' as they handed me a big hamper full of all sorts of toys and food.

'Make a wish,' they cried, 'and it will be answered.'

I wished for my husband to come home.

The very next day he arrived. No, he wasn't better but he had managed to travel miles home by train because, he said, 'I had a message from you on New Year's Eve. I heard your voice and knew I would never see you all again if I didn't come.' He had entreated the doctor to let him come home. He knew that he was dying and wanted us to have those last days together.

Ever since then I have always made sure that I made someone else's New Year's Eve brighter. A happy new year is waiting around the corner and nobody can tell me otherwise.

Once we have some idea what the future will bring, at least we know what we're up against and can prepare but waiting for the unknown can be one of the most scary things. Help us, Lord, not to feel so threatened that, like Naomi, we focus on past troubles, becoming weighed down by bitterness as we stand on the brink of the unknown. Help us instead to focus and draw strength from the signs that we're not alone – the kindness of unexpected people who stand with us, a ray of light which you send through the swirling darkness as a sign of your presence . . . Help us, like Ruth and Margaret, to support those who wait for an uncertain future, alone, in the cold and the dark. Show us how to bring them some cheer.

* * *

Waiting for . . . *each other*

When you come together, it is not the Lord's Supper you eat, for as you eat, each of you goes ahead without waiting for anybody else. One remains hungry, another gets drunk. Don't you have homes to eat and drink in? Or do you despise the church of God and humiliate those who have nothing? What shall I say to you? Shall I praise you for this? Certainly not! So then, my brothers, when you come together to eat, wait for each other.
(1 Corinthians 11.20–22, 33)

I'm an 'early' person who doesn't like waiting, especially for food. If I'm invited out for 7.30, annoyingly I arrive at 7.30, maybe even 7.25. If I ask friends round for a meal at 7.30, what I mean is that I will be serving up dinner at 7.30 – and if they've not arrived by 7.50 I'm phoning them, the police and the fire service, while dinner ruins on the stove. When first married, in my twenties I gave one set of late-arriving guests an earful – enough to put them off their already dried-up food and ruin the evening. By now, I've more or less learned to add on at least half an hour and invite people around at 7.00, on the grounds that then we can eat at 7.30. Except that the time of 7.00 sticks in my head and I start cooking early and fretting that they won't arrive . . .

I have a nasty feeling that Jesus and I wouldn't have got on very well in this respect. He must have been late more often than not. He'd be stopping to pray, to chat with some lost soul or to heal a poor beggar. I wonder if those women who cooked for him sometimes – Martha? Joanna? – ever fumed about burnt dinners?

Now the situation is reversed. It's Jesus who invites us to his special meal – and the least we can do is to wait for one another. Wait for the person in the wheelchair who couldn't get through the door at the last minute because everyone else was trying to do the same thing. Wait for dear old Mabel who's becoming a bit slow and has probably forgotten that it's Sunday again. Wait for Ben whose wife of sixty years died last week; he's hiding in the toilets, feeling too emotional to face us all at the moment. Wait for the worship leader who wants us to sing something through 'just one more time'. Wait for that Katey and her five kids when the rota for giving them all a lift to church must have gone wrong again, so could someone please go and find them? Sigh. Can't we just get on with it – after all, we're busy people!

Do we ever become so caught up in the petty hitches of life, even church life, that we forget what's really important – our relationships with Jesus and with one another?

Sylvia Herbert, a retired teacher of French and Spanish, showed me a light-hearted poem which she wrote about waiting. It made me think that, when we're waiting for those we really love, they take precedence. Whether independent child, partner or even cat, his or her schedule becomes more important than our own. Provided we can let go and avoid being 'clingy' there's joy in the anticipation even when our waiting goes unrecognized.

My cat comes in
rattling the flap of his special door
to say he's back

from his wanderings
and ready to check his filled blue dish, hungry
for breakfast.

A morning to sleep,
then click through the flap; he's clocking out
for lunchtime patrol.

Over the rough lawn
under the spiky hawthorn hedge he crawls, and
out of sight.

The flap won't sound
again for an hour or maybe more,
so I shall rest.

It's six o'clock,
I'm busy cooking in the kitchen now,
and listening.

I look out for him,
he should have returned a while ago;
no cat-flap noise

to herald his entry.
The house is full of alien sounds.
His door stays shut.

A sudden rattle
as my cat bursts in, and I pretend
he isn't late at all.

Sylvia Herbert

From cat-flaps to the sublime – John the Baptist said these words when at last he met Jesus, 'The friend who attends the bridegroom waits and listens for him, and is full of joy when he hears the bridegroom's voice. That joy is mine, and it is now complete. He must become greater; I must become less' (John 3.29–30). Lord, help us to have that same attitude when we meet you in one another – an attitude of joyful anticipation and of putting the other person, their needs and schedule, before ourselves.

*   *   *

Waiting for . . . *family members*

They went up out of Egypt and came to their father Jacob in the land of Canaan. They told him, 'Joseph is still alive! In fact, he is ruler of all Egypt.'

Jacob was stunned; he did not believe them. But when they told him everything Joseph had said to them, and when he saw the carts Joseph had sent to carry him back, the spirit of their father Jacob revived and . . . said, 'I'm convinced! My son Joseph is still alive. I will go and see him before I die.'

. . . Joseph had his chariot made ready and went to Goshen to meet his father Israel. As soon as Joseph appeared before him, he threw his arms around his father and wept for a long time. Israel said to Joseph, 'Now I am ready to die, since I have seen for myself that you are still alive.'

(Genesis 45.25–28; 46.29–30)

54

What a complex, sorry family saga, beating anything in *East-Enders*. A widowed father favours a boastful, arrogant dreamer of a teenager over his other eleven sons, making this clear by an ostentatious gift. Jealous older brothers attempt murder, then betray their young sibling into slavery, their lies about his demise plunging Dad into grief without resolution. The brothers show an assortment of 'interesting' sexual proclivities such as sleeping with Dad's concubine, or with a daughter-in-law (mistaking her for a prostitute). Meanwhile the enslaved dreamer-brother gains influence in a foreign land, then roller-coasts downwards as he is wrongfully imprisoned. Released, he becomes Pharaoh's right-hand man when his dreams save Egypt from starving to death in a famine that affects the whole region. Ten of the brothers, going to beg food from Egypt, fail to recognize the young dreamer while he, desperate to see his younger brother and his father, tricks them into returning. They fear for their lives but he forgives, all ends happily and God's chosen people – who will emerge from this unlikely, dysfunctional family – live to breed and prosper for at least a generation, until the next crisis.

Millennia later, families remain complex. Tensions abound. Mistakes, lies, betrayals, unfairness and wrongdoing echo down the years. Just as Dad (Jacob, aka Israel) had to wait many grief-filled years before expressing himself content to die in his long-lost son's arms, so parents today wait in powerless agony for offspring who have gone off the rails – or offspring wait for a parent who has left home and lost touch. Yet for those who wait in any century, grace, forgiveness and reconciliation may come. Sue Shaw works for Victim Support. Here she writes about her own adoptive mother, Blanche.

Blanche and Harry fell in love in 1939. She was just fifteen and he was twenty-four. Because of her age they were married by special licence. A few weeks later Harry was called up for active service and spent the next six years stationed in the Far East.

On his return they settled down in their first home, hoping to start a family. Blanche longed to be a mum. The years passed but no children came along.

After being married for fourteen years they adopted Susan, who was eleven months old. This was a great success, so much so that the following year they adopted another little girl, Elaine, a year younger. Blanche doted on them. However by the time they were six and five respectively the marriage was in deep trouble and Blanche discovered she was pregnant to another man.

Scared and confused, Blanche agonized over what to do for the best. In desperation she packed her bags and ran away, unable to explain her plight to the girls. She settled in Wales where she gave birth to her child. It was stillborn.

The couple divorced and their father was given custody of the girls. The years passed. Every birthday and Christmas she sent cards and wrote long letters to each of the girls. She longed to see them again and hoped that one day the girls might make contact.

In her fifties Blanche developed cancer of the spine, leaving her in great pain and discomfort. One morning quite unexpectedly her youngest daughter Elaine, who by then was sixteen years old, turned up at her door. It was a wonderful and emotional reunion.

Elaine returned home, thrilled that they had been able to meet and talk together. The very next day Blanche died, knowing she had been granted one of her prayers. Her waiting was over.

You might like to use the words of St Paul to pray for those you know who are going through a painful time of waiting for those they love, especially for family members.

For this reason I bow my knees before the Father, from whom every family in heaven and on earth is named, that according to the riches of his glory he may grant you to be strengthened with might through his Spirit in the inner man, and that Christ may dwell in your hearts through faith; that you, being rooted and grounded in love, may have power to comprehend with all the saints what is the breadth and length and height and depth, and to know the love of Christ which surpasses knowledge, that you may be filled with all the fulness of God. Now to him who by the power at work within us is able to do far more abundantly than all that we ask or think, to him be glory in the church and in Christ Jesus to all generations, for ever and ever. Amen.

(Ephesians 3.14–21, RSV)

* * *

Waiting for . . . *one another – patience*

As a prisoner for the Lord, then, I urge you to live a life worthy of the calling you have received. Be completely humble and gentle; be patient, bearing with one another in love. Make every effort to keep the unity of the Spirit through the bond of peace. (Ephesians 4.1–3)

A friend and her arthritic husband went on holiday with another couple. She told me afterwards how delighted she was when they waited for her husband, kept pace with him. That wouldn't have been me; selfishly I'd have wanted to dash ahead, seeing all that was to be seen. I like to go at my own pace. That's why I was reluctant to research what the Bible has to say about patience, though I knew I must, for this book on waiting.

If the Church is meant to be a caring community, waiting patiently for one another isn't optional. We won't be united if I'm here with the quicker ones and the slowcoaches are over there. (I wonder if that's why Jesus said the first shall be last and the last shall be first?) At the moment my back's hurting, reminding me that quick ones become slow sometimes. In the NRSV, Psalm 73.15 says, 'If I had said, "I will talk on in this [negative] way", I would have been untrue to the circle of your children.' Most other versions translate 'circle' as 'generation' but I prefer to picture a circle of people with linked arms. At any one time some may be flagging, others vigorous – but the circle will hold everyone up if we stick together, even if our patience contains tension.

A loose, passive, floppy people-circle isn't strong: better if there's a certain tension, if people are leaning outwards slightly, for example. As you will have gathered by now, I love to facilitate the telling of other people's stories, and stories can't do without tension either. Sometimes I hear a brilliant one, only to be told, 'Please keep that confidential. We can't put it in a book, not yet, because it would hurt sister/father/friend . . .' So you too are going to have to wait patiently for these wonderful stories. Now there's some creative tension for you!

What can the creative tension contained within patience do? Sarah Williams, a costume-designer and mother of school-age children writes of a time when she waited for someone:

When she knocked on my door it was Christmas; I barely knew her yet I sensed something was wrong. Within minutes our friendship was sealed. As her tears flowed she relayed the whole story and I reassured her that I would be there, for her and the children.

It must have seemed to my friend as our relationship developed, that while her life had come crashing down since the swift departure of her husband, mine was enviably intact. It was too soon to let her know that I also had patiently rebuilt my life many times over. 'If I can just get through this first year . . .' she would say to me, but I knew in my heart it would take five.

Slowly painful days built into more hopeful weeks, bit by bit she ticked off the months. I was right, the process proved to be agonizingly protracted for her. A quick-witted, intelligent woman, she was used to moving at a swifter pace. But her belief system had been shattered, followed by a mind and body collapse; this person needed time to recover. Steadily she emerged out of the dark and began, tentatively, to embrace the day.

Then came the custody battles, interviews with social workers, the sessions in court, the agonizing wait for their verdicts. Back down the road of recovery she would retreat, only to pick herself up again, surprising me with her resilience.

Gradually I observed a change, a spiritual shift; she started to let go a bit, handing over the controls to powers beyond her. Then the healing really kicked in.

It has been three years of tortuous waiting, rewriting a life that was, to a life that is. My friend now lives in the moment. No longer fiercely independent, she allows others to assist her. Now she can offer them support too.

During the long wait for her mind and body to function properly again, she and I both observed her rediscovering what had previously been hidden from her. That is her true self.

Lord, while we often struggle with patience, you bring good, creative things out of the tension of waiting. You are the true storyteller, the master of pace, for groups as well as individuals!

* * *

Waiting for . . . *a very long time*

Hang on!

How long, O LORD? Will you forget me for ever? How long will you hide your face from me? How long must I wrestle with my thoughts and every day have sorrow in my heart? How long will my enemy triumph over me? Look on me and answer, O Lord my God. Give light to my eyes, or I will sleep in death; my enemy will say, 'I have overcome him,' and my foes will rejoice when I fall.

But I trust in your unfailing love; my heart rejoices in your salvation. I will sing to the Lord, for he has been good to me.

(Psalm 13)

Waiting for a bus, in the cold or rain, an hour can seem to last for ever. But of course that's my impatience speaking. How ridiculous – an hour, or two, even days or months aren't anything like for ever.

On the news we hear of Christians suffering terrible injustice under oppressive regimes for years, in prison perhaps, with loved ones 'disappeared' or killed.

Those can seem far away but this long-term waiting was brought home to me when the deputy head of what had been my children's junior school appeared on the television. It seemed that, one 'ordinary' day, her teenage daughter went out and failed to return home. Years on, despite all kinds of efforts, appeals and searches, she remains one more 'missing person'. I can't begin to imagine what that kind of unresolved agony is like for her family.

For a Christian, waiting long-term, other painful questions arise. Why is God not responding? Has he forgotten me? What's happened to our relationship when I need him? I can't see his face or hear his voice anymore! This is no time for games of hide-and-seek, Lord! Destroying me and those that I love isn't going to bring glory to your name!

I'm struck by the psalmist's honesty. And yet the final two sentences don't appear to follow on from the rest – suddenly he's trusting in God's love, salvation and goodness, even singing and rejoicing. There's a huge logical gap here some-where, but then relationships never were logical. Somewhere in that gap between his honest cries of hurt and his declarations of praise and joy, the psalmist met with God. Even though his questions weren't answered and his circumstances remained unchanged, he saw things from a completely different per-spective. For one thing he remembered all the good that God had done in the past.

Do we have to be damaged by long waits in terrible cir-cumstances as people often are? Something else on the news humbled and moved me to tears last night. A woman's bent and ancient fingers teased such feeling from piano keys. Only music had saved pianist Alice Herz-Sommer (though not her husband) from dying during two terrible years in a Nazi con-centration camp. Now aged 103 and living in a tiny north-London flat, she told the reporter fluently with a Czech accent how rich and fortunate she felt – as only those can, she said, who have lived with nothing, not even food.

Stephanie Hüsler is a recording artist, vocal coach, language teacher and writer. Originally from the USA, she lives in Zurich, Switzerland, with her husband Stefan.

I was sitting in my office at home when I heard news that numbed my senses. A terrible accident – my cousin was lying in a coma and her two young daughters, one aged three years, the other seven months, were both gone, their lives snuffed out in an instant.

Three days later, flying over the Atlantic, my tears of grief finally responded. I'd only recently begun email correspondence with this cousin, after years of living separate lives. When I landed in Kansas, my home state of so many years ago, my first reunion with family was at the graveside of a double children's funeral. No one should have to experience such sorrow but, through those days, I did feel God's peace carrying me. And then the waiting began. That was August 1999, and to this day my cousin hovers in a coma.

The questions come, ever more persistently: Why? How long? When? Questions we could no more answer than we could catch the wind, but something in our human nature struggles to capture the answers, longs to make sense of the senseless, all the same. God's ways are higher than our ways – it's something we've all heard, but when the test of our trust comes it is only then that we truly learn the depth of its significance – and through it all God is gentle and faithful, whether we understand it or not.

We go through various stages of waiting: the impatience, the frustration, the anger, the casting blame. But eventually, if we let him, God will bring peace into our waiting. It can become an act of faith, and then *active faith*, if we let go and let God.

> Lord, only you can bring
> peace in the waiting,
> presence in the absence,
> joy through the agony,
> hope through the despair.

* * *

Waiting for . . . *hope deferred*

Now there was a man in Jerusalem called Simeon, who was righteous and devout. He was waiting for the consolation of Israel, and the Holy Spirit was upon him. It had been revealed to him by the Holy Spirit that he would not die before he had seen the Lord's Christ. (Luke 2.25–26)

It sounds as though Simeon was old and had been waiting to see God's promise fulfilled for a very long time. In the end, before he died, he had the extraordinary experience of holding the Son of God in his arms, in the form of what looked like a perfectly normal baby boy. At that moment he knew that this little one would bring not exactly 'consolation' to his nation but 'glory' and 'the falling and rising of many in Israel'. Even more, he would be 'a light of revelation to the Gentiles'.

Bystanders in the temple courts might have thought not much had happened but Simeon knew differently – knew that he had done his part, not only praying over the years but now, at a pivotal moment in history, he had recognized hope. To him and to others who had eyes to see, eternity had become visible and tangible in this space–time world, and would change everything. The old man could now 'depart in peace'.

I don't suppose my village is unusual in that there are a number of people in its churches who, like Simeon, are righteous, devout and full of God's Spirit. Yet they have been waiting and longing for years and years for their much-loved spouses to come to know Jesus' grace for themselves. Many of the not-yet-Christians are delightful people, who join in all kinds of things with the church community, help out their neighbours and are loving, kind, giving and commendable in every way. You would think they are model disciples, but they will deny, very firmly, that they are following Christ. Their Christian partners gather together to pray on occasions, but as time goes by and nothing seems to change, their sadness grows. As Proverbs 13.12 says, 'Hope deferred makes the heart sick, but a longing fulfilled is a tree of life.' Will that moment never come when the light of eternity will become evident to those they love, sparking faith into life, changing everything? Whichever way you look at it, things aren't easy – but there is encouragement in Jenny Goddard's story.

Jenny married Ron Goddard while still in her teens. At first they went to church together, but Ron preferred Sunday morning digs with the archaeological society. Such a good man, he was always helping others, so Jenny wasn't too bothered until, in 1970, they moved to Surrey. There, Jean and Mike, neighbours and members of Jenny's new church, became friends. The Holy Spirit lit up Jenny's faith in a new way after Jean prayed with her. Feeling that Ron was missing out, she asked if he believed in God and was shocked when he replied, 'No. I'm happy for you to believe what you want but I won't risk destroying your faith by discussing spiritual matters.' She and other good Christian friends kept praying and taking opportunities but Jenny knew she had to be wise. During the Blitz, Ron had been confirmed, along with other children, while they were evacuated to a camp in Hindhead. 'People were kind there and I enjoyed learning things by heart,' he said, later. But childhood hurts made him fear being vulnerable, especially before God. His father had been a dreadful man, leaving the family in abject poverty, even homeless, once – and the children were in and out of care. Remarkably, Ron went on to become a chemist, a world-renowned expert in the packaging industry and a wonderful husband and father.

As the years went by Jenny's great hopes that Ron would come to share her faith changed to a deepening sadness and a lack of any assurance. She kept praying and taking opportunities but, 'I always worried that I could have done better,' she said. 'The way Ron lived put me to shame. He came through his difficult childhood with such fine qualities and never bore any grudge. I couldn't bear the thought that if he died without Christ it would all be for nothing.'

Then, just before Christmas 1998, a massive pain in Jenny's head had Ron rushing her to the doctor. In the car her heart stopped. She slumped forward. Suddenly everything was light. She felt wonderful . . . but was clinically dead – until the doctor rushed out into the car park and revived her. Jenny came round in his surgery, in terrible pain. During the next few weeks in a neurological hospital she had a vision where she could choose to die. On choosing life, she was told it would be 'a long hard road'.

Few people recover from such a serious brain haemorrhage, yet Ron wouldn't make himself vulnerable by facing up to Jenny's mortality. He was struck by the way Christians cared, though. 'Everybody loves you,' he said.

'And they love you too,' Jenny replied. Deeds speak louder than words.

In the spring of 2003, on the motorway to Stansted Airport, a lorry hit the car just where Ron was sitting, spun it round and left it wrecked on the hard shoulder. Miraculously they survived to go on their walking holiday to Cyprus. Yet Ron returned home jaundiced. He died of cancer of the pancreas at home on Christmas Eve, spending much of the intervening time in hospital.

During those pain-filled months he came to terms with his own and Jenny's vulnerability. The hospital staff and chaplains were so kind and Ron liked to go to the chapel when well enough. Jenny spent every day with him. At 8 p.m. he would say, 'Let's have a prayer before you go.' Then one evening he phoned her at 10 p.m. 'I feared the worst', Jenny told me, 'then dissolved into tears when he said, "I thought you'd want to know that I visited the chapel after you left. I've such a sense of peace. I know everything's all right now." I told him that was the peace of God which passes all understanding. After that Ron would be praying for me. And I had so much to tell him, to explain.' But how, oh how, would she live without him?

'God will care for you,' he assured her, thanking God for her and the family.

At the end Jenny was looking after Ron at home with the help of hospice nurses but he was ministering to her spiritually.

'It certainly was – still is – the long, hard road that I was promised,' Jenny said. 'But God sees the deepest desires of our hearts – and through slow steps and many people, Ron came to faith.'

If, like Jenny, you've been waiting for something for years and years, so that you're beginning to lose faith in yourself as well as in God, take this promise to heart, declare it out loud and make it yours.

> For in him you have been enriched in every way – in all your speaking and in all your knowledge – because our testimony about Christ was confirmed in you. Therefore you do not lack any spiritual gift as you eagerly wait for our Lord Jesus Christ to be revealed. He will keep you strong to the end, so that you will be blameless on the day of our Lord Jesus Christ. God, who has called you into fellowship with his Son Jesus Christ our Lord, is faithful. (1 Corinthians 1.5–9)

Waiting as . . .

Working with wood I've learned to be patient. I learned the carpentry trade from my father. 'Joseph,' he would say. 'Let the wood set the pace of your work, never rush at it. Whether you're using the saw or the adze, the plane or the chisel. And from time to time pause, stretch your back and sharpen your tools. You'll find that at the end of the day you will have got through more work than if you had gone steadily on without a break.' And I shall tell my son the same. Whether you're making a bed or a table, a chest or a chair, let the pieces come together in their own time.

I had to learn to wait for my wife, Mary. We were so in love and we wanted to come together and enjoy our love. But we waited. Mind you we had both been visited by angels; and that's something very special. Yes, we waited until our first child was born.

Then, you'll remember, Herod sent his soldiers to slaughter all the children two years old and under. How our hearts bled for them. An angel warned us of this and we travelled to Egypt and waited again until Herod died and it was safe to return to our own country.

Jesus is a young man now, a fine carpenter with a good eye and strong, skilled hands. But sometimes I see a faraway look in his eyes. When he is not working he studies our scriptures a lot; I just have a feeling that he won't be a carpenter much longer, he is waiting for something too.

(Eric Leat)

The glory that will be revealed in us

I consider that our present sufferings are not worth comparing with the glory that will be revealed in us . . . We know that the whole creation has been groaning as in the pains of childbirth right up to the present time . . . In this hope we were saved. But hope that is seen is no hope at all. Who hopes for what he already has? But if we hope for what we do not yet have, we wait for it patiently . . . The Spirit helps us in our weakness. We do not know what we ought to pray for, but the Spirit himself intercedes for us with groans that words cannot express . . . And we know that in all things God works for the good of those who love him, who have been called according to his purpose.

(Romans 8.18–28)

Paul's words aren't glib – the Roman Christians' sufferings were considerably more than our own; they waited with an urgency on which hung life or death. Their hope in a God who was 'working for their good' was being tested to the limit as they lived under persecution.

There's not much to see in the early stages of pregnancy either – sickness and tiredness perhaps. You have to invest the full nine months, the uncertainty, the danger (much more acute to both mother and child in Paul's day) and finally the pains and sheer hard work of labour before you see much more than a swollen front.

If God has in mind 'the glory that will be revealed in us' – if that's what is being 'born' in us, then no wonder the 'pregnancy' can seem long, complicated and painful sometimes. We may think we know what to pray for, the direction in which God wants us to head, just as a pregnant woman might be convinced she's having a boy – until a little girl is born. Waiting, with God, involves surprises as well as frustrations.

Often only on looking back can we see what good surprises they were.

Hilary Creed, a retired teacher from Bromley, Kent, wrote this about what she thought was a great disappointment.

The letter said, 'You are on the waiting list for this university.' So I waited.

'It's a test of faith,' I told myself. 'At the last minute I'll hear that I can train as a social worker.'

At length the letter came – they regretted there was no place for me. I went for consolation to a Christian teacher who'd watched me grow in faith and commitment. 'The bottom has fallen out of my world,' I wailed.

'Nonsense!' she said. 'God has a purpose in it.'

And so he had. I was too late to apply elsewhere, so embarked on a secretarial course at the local technical college, where we began a Christian Union. Eight long months of struggling with shorthand and the agony of typing in time to music opened the door to a secretarial job, helping the elderly in Greater London.

When I did eventually train, not in social work but as a teacher, the typing skills proved invaluable and have been ever since, used in every part of my life, saving me hours of time, and – a great bonus – making the transition to computers much less terrifying, and drafting and editing stories a joy.

I would have failed as a social worker. Those short months of waiting and preparation changed the direction of my life and enabled me to cope with nearly thirty years of teaching. Also to run activities at a Christian group and on residential holidays for forty years, to embark on writing books and, most importantly, to keep greatly valued friendships alive, one made during my time at the tech.

Now I'm constantly grateful for the gift of that brief waiting and preparation time. It has enriched my life and, above all, reinforced my trust in his promise that 'all things work together for good to those who love God'.

Lord, for all who wait weighed down by acute disappointment, sickness, dread, pain or fear, let them hear the Spirit's groans on their behalf. Let them feel your overwhelming love as you invest in them. Let them glimpse something of the glory ahead.

* * *

Waiting as . . . *investment in what's eternal*

But you, dear friends, build yourselves up in your most holy faith and pray in the Holy Spirit. Keep yourselves in God's love as you wait for the mercy of our Lord Jesus Christ to bring you to eternal life. Be merciful to those who doubt.

(Jude 20–22)

For a maximum of one month I had cancer – perhaps the easiest kind to remove, completely. The worst aspect for me, despite the NHS acting faster than a rocket, was certainly the waiting.

A couple of hours after being told I had a precancerous condition and would need major surgery, I was meant to be leading our church home group. I got through it because, right at the start, my dear friend Marina sat down and played the piano spontaneously, from her heart, her spirit. She made me feel God's presence and peace in that room and it lasted for the rest of the evening. Afterwards, I knew I should be keeping myself in God's love and building myself up in my faith. But it was fear, not faith, that built. Panic kept me awake at night. By day I rushed about trying to arrange things that were impossible to plan. Occasionally I did manage to pray in the

Holy Spirit – if only because I couldn't even begin to pray in my own strength.

Conscious that many people were praying, caring and full of faith for me, I was only too aware that I wasn't waiting anywhere near as well as a mature Christian 'should'. I must have been a pain and am so grateful that the wait was short and above all that God (and other Christians) are merciful to those who doubt. I did learn though that the Lord is capable of keeping us in his love, mercy and life eternal, even when we do everything wrong. Humans could never have planned this, but my daughter 'happened' to be available to look after us when I came out of hospital and 'happened' to have just acquired exactly the right experience to run both my weekly writing groups and a planned book-launch evening.

I had an easily removable cancer for perhaps a month; Rachel Gilbert has suffered with stomach cancer for six years. Despite a life full of pain and hospital visits, she tries to enjoy every day that she has. Those who know her say that she is a lovely girl to be around. Now twenty and very ill, facing the difficult decision of whether she should risk having major surgery, she wrote this, about waiting for God.

Well, what exactly am I waiting for? I'm sitting in my room all alone in the dark; my eyes are tight shut and my hands are clasped in the prayer position.

You see I have just said my first prayer ever, other than the usual casual wishes. This was a big proper prayer. The problem is I'm not sure what I'm waiting for now. Is there going to be a big flash of light, a new strange voice in my head or is it simpler than that? I have no idea. I'm waiting for the sign that means everything is going to be all right again and I'm not sure I can wait too long for it to happen. Surely seeing as I haven't said a proper prayer before I should have some extra points stacked up somewhere? I mean some people pray ten times a day, so surely I'm owed something for my first go!

I sit there still with my eyes tight shut and my hands in the same position but nothing happens, no voices, no flashes of light, just silence, pure chilling silence. Slowly, I dare to open my eyes but nothing has changed. My room, my bed and my furniture look exactly the same. I look around me and check there are no notes dropped from heaven but then I realize that it is simpler than that. You have to believe. You have to truly put yourself and all your worries into the Lord's hands. It's not an instant answer; you have to wait and sometimes you think that nothing is happening but what you haven't noticed is that little things are changing slowly which are putting you in the right direction. The true answer is faith in what the Lord does and what the Lord is.

Thank you, Lord, that our faith is built up more in the bad times than the good, even though it doesn't always feel that way at the time. Thank you that all this waiting is often more about who you are – and who we are – than about what you or we do, or fail to do. Help us to 'turn to your direction', to see things from your perspective, a little more every day. Help us to pray in the Spirit for those who wait in difficult circumstances, perhaps using the final words of Jude's letter:

To him who is able to keep you from falling and to present you before his glorious presence without fault and with great joy – to the only God our Saviour be glory, majesty, power and authority, through Jesus Christ our Lord, before all ages, now and for evermore! Amen.   (Jude 24–25)

*   *   *

Building community as *we wait for one another*

> The LORD is the everlasting God,
> the Creator of the ends of the earth.
> He does not faint or grow weary,
> his understanding is unsearchable.
> He gives power to the faint,
> and to him who has no might he increases strength.
> Even youths shall faint and be weary,
> and young men shall fall exhausted;
> but they who wait for the LORD shall renew their strength,
> they shall mount up with wings like eagles,
> they shall run and not be weary,
> they shall walk and not faint.
>
> (Isaiah 40.28–31, RSV)

God invests in us if we let him. On the cross, Jesus offered us his strength for our weakness, his life for our mortality, his righteousness for our sinfulness, his joy for our sorrow, his health for our sickness, his freedom for our captivity and oppression. Paradoxically, this once-for-all-time investment goes on every day, every hour, every minute. Unlike us, Father, Son and Holy Spirit never grow weary, have all the time in the world and are expert at waiting. That is just as well since, as with sunshine's investment into a glacier, sometimes it takes time for us to benefit – to melt and change as individuals and even more, as communities. Think of the long, slow progress of Christians' fight against slavery, or world poverty . . .

Has God invested one of his dreams in you, be it big or small? If so, you'll need not only your own perseverance but the strength that God will keep giving you for the long haul. Some, like Abraham, may find that years have gone by with only frustration and restless wanderings to show for the dream – as though

God has lit a fire in an old steam engine and stoked it to bring water to the boil when there appear to be no tracks leading anywhere. But if we spend some of that restlessness, that head of steam in waiting on the Lord, something will be happening, slowly, within us, preparing us.

Mary Mills, a teacher and writer from Barrow-on-Trent, Derbyshire, tells the story of one of God's African investments which is yielding his kind of profit for affluent Western Christians as they learn so much from their new 'family'. They've joined with Ugandans in building something more than a hostel – a community across the continents, sharing their relationship with Jesus, their compassion, sorrowing and rejoicing together.

'I have a dream . . .' – the immortal words of Martin Luther King, borrowed by my Ugandan pastor friend, Revd Samuel Wasswa.

'I have a dream – that we will build a hostel, fill it with Ugandan Christian university students, and the rent they pay for accommodation will be used to support the widowed mothers and the orphans with AIDS on our project.'

That was five years ago – and slowly but surely it is taking shape. Patient Africans are used to waiting.

Waiting – for funds to trickle in for the cost of the land.

Waiting – for funds for the foundations.

Waiting – for the mud bricks to bake before starting to build the walls.

Waiting – for the rains to finish so the barefoot workers can work in dry conditions.

Waiting – for funds to pay them.

Waiting – for funds for the roofing timbers, door shutters, iron roofing sheets.

Waiting – for funds to dig the pit latrine.

Waiting – for funds to buy concrete for the floors, plaster for the walls, paint to finish the job.

Waiting – for funds to get the electricity connected and water supplies laid on.

Waiting – on the part of the students, anxious to find good accommodation at a reasonable rent.

All this waiting – dependent on trickling funds from the rich West to the struggling poor in the heart of Africa.

One big cheque could have seen the job done years ago. And yet throughout the waiting and campaigning, hearts and minds have been touched and awareness raised to a far bigger audience. Who knows where this may lead?

The longer the wait, the greater the appreciation of the realization of the dream.

Now, with the end in sight, we await the grand opening. Hallelujah!

The joyful celebrations in Africa will be shared by all their supporters in the West.

God's timing is perfect – and love *is* patient.

Spend some time waiting on God, enjoying his presence, listening to him instead of talking. What is the part he has for you in his dream of building creative, harmonious, loving communities? Let him minister his grace into those stopped or ultra-slow-moving things which wear you down, especially where they involve other people.

* * *

Waiting as . . . *preparation for when 'all the buses come at once'*

Moses . . . fled to Midian, where he settled as a foreigner and had two sons. After forty years had passed, an angel appeared to Moses in the flames of a burning bush in the desert near Mount Sinai . . . 'I am the God of your fathers, the God of

Abraham, Isaac and Jacob.' Moses trembled with fear and did not dare to look.

Then the Lord said to him, 'Take off your sandals; the place where you are standing is holy ground. I have indeed seen the oppression of my people in Egypt. I have heard their groaning and have come down to set them free . . .'

[Moses] led them out of Egypt and did wonders and miraculous signs in Egypt, at the Red Sea and for forty years in the desert. (Acts 7.29–34, 36)

Moses had a long wait – most of it spent away from his own people, from his mission and destiny and from his God. First came his youth in Pharaoh's court, then forty of his middle years passed as shepherd, husband and father in the household of a priest of an alien religion in an obscure country. After the dramatic, holy encounter with God at the burning bush you could say that the desert of his life burst into sudden and spectacular bloom. Or, in the speech of a few millennia later, that 'all his buses came at once'.

Even after the 'mission impossible' of leading his people away from oppression in Egypt, Moses had to keep them together, true to their new identity of nationhood under God, and keep them on track in the wilderness for another forty years. He had to learn how to delegate authority, listen to God, uphold the law, feed the people and . . . I have the feeling that God could have done with several Moseses.

Reading the Bible throws up plenty more examples of people who waited for years before all their buses came at once – David, Joshua, Esther, Jesus himself . . . You might want to read the stories of how they coped and what they learned, in the waiting times and in the heat of action. Their waiting certainly built up heads of steam, to power whatever needed to be done.

Waiting as . . .

Moses' life changed when he saw a bush burning. I want to tell you the story of my friend Marina Jurjevic who, following a different sign, embarked on a mission for which she needs a huge amount of commitment, energy, creativity and love. Back in her native Croatia, Marina worked in finance. Then she moved to the UK because her husband moved from Croatia to work with my husband in Surrey. She writes of Croatia:

> I worked from day to day, without a sense of time, like music without pause or painting without white places to rest your gaze. That lasted too long, I felt.
> I knew I had to break the circle and start to live again.
> And I did it.
> New beginnings . . . UK.
> I walked from day to day by the river, without a sense of time – with a day divided in time – before lunch, long walks and evening . . .

It was at least a year before she managed to relax. She needed that time. Having read one of my books and experienced something of Jesus at a Christian conference centre, Marina began to meet with him down by the river near her flat. Due to certain experiences in Croatia she'd had a poor opinion of him but now her spirit had room to breathe. Something came to birth in her, though her life remained quiet. She continues:

> One day, during my regular walks by the river, an old man ran towards me, euphoric. 'I saw him!' He pointed to the river.
> 'Who did you see?' I asked.
> 'A kingfisher!'
> I still remember the amazing shine in his blue eyes, the utter happiness. I smiled . . . What a special moment, I thought. Certainly it must be a special bird, I knew, although I had never seen it.

Peaceful days passed. Then, completely unexpectedly, I saw that beautiful blueness flashing above the water's surface. I knew immediately that it was a kingfisher.

An amazing peacefulness and joy came into me, this was something special.

On my way back home I saw a little advert posted in a shop window, asking for volunteers. I wrote down the telephone number. Back home, I had no idea who I was calling, nor what they did.

The volunteer coordinator asked if I had any experience of working with people with disabilities, such as visual impairment and learning difficulties.

'None,' I said.

But she gave me first an information pack then an interview. She showed me the centre at the busiest time, when all the groups were together in the lounge having tea. When one individual started to jump and shout I just knew that I wanted to come back here as a volunteer helper. 'Thank you!' I said in my thoughts to God.

I had so much to learn it was breathtaking. After six months I applied for a job (the regulations having changed so that I could now be in paid employment) and became a full-time team member. This work has been invaluable to me, teaching me to re-evaluate everything about life. The wonderful people I work with taught me to change the standard ways of perception and communication. They inspired me to share what we have and to challenge the stereotypes. I am endlessly thankful for this experience. This is not an easy work and it has certainly brought me closer to God.

After three years I reduced my hours so that I could study art. I had been using art and music in my work at the centre, and my work continues to influence my art, which I see as enabling me to communicate in a non-standard way, going beyond words and vision, language and intelligence.

These days Marina's creative as well as caring side keeps her amazingly busy. As one of her projects for art college she asked sixty-nine people to do some artwork for her, including friends from the centre, from the UK, Croatia and many other countries. She asked children and old people, sighted and blind, philosophy professors and adults with learning disabilities. Whether professionals and students in the art world or complete beginners, people came together to enjoy each other's work at the exhibition. Suddenly Marina is being asked to run workshops for arts students in Croatia, raising awareness of visually impaired people and encouraging different perceptions of visual art. She has such a God-given gift in that area. It's a long way from the world of finance. 'From my old life, I never could have imagined this could happen!' After that quiet year all her buses have certainly come at once! But Marina says: 'These days, I occasionally see a kingfisher by the river. He always brings that desired peacefulness and strength to me. I feel, when I go to the river, that I go to meet with God . . .'

These are some of Marina's favourite verses from the Bible. You might like to meditate on them, whether you're in a waiting time or a busy time at the moment.

> There is a time for everything, and a season for every activity under heaven:
> a time to be born and a time to die, a time to plant and a time to uproot,
> a time to kill and a time to heal, a time to tear down and a time to build,
> a time to weep and a time to laugh, a time to mourn and a time to dance,
> a time to scatter stones and a time to gather them, a time to embrace and a time to refrain,
> a time to search and a time to give up, a time to keep and a time to throw away,

a time to tear and a time to mend, a time to be silent and a
time to speak,
a time to love and a time to hate, a time for war and a time
for peace . . .
He has made everything beautiful in its time. He has also set
eternity in the hearts of men; yet they cannot fathom what
God has done from beginning to end. I know that there
is nothing better for men than to be happy and do good
while they live.

(Ecclesiastes 3.1–12)

* * *

Waiting as . . . *robbery*

Waiting *as* . . . disappointment

Do not trust a neighbour; put no confidence in a friend. Even
with her who lies in your embrace be careful of your words.
For a son dishonours his father, a daughter rises up against
her mother, a daughter-in-law against her mother-in-law – a
man's enemies are the members of his own household. But as
for me, I watch in hope for the LORD, I wait for God my Saviour;
my God will hear me. Do not gloat over me, my enemy! Though
I have fallen, I will rise. Though I sit in darkness, the LORD will
be my light. (Micah 7.5–8)

What's implied here? Waiting – note the future tense. And the
message? 'Don't trust people: instead watch, hope and pray.'
That's not the way God meant it to be but sadly, for many
people, guilty or innocent, that's the lesson learned. Waiting
for people in eager expectation can turn to disappointment.
Even some fine Christian leaders, people of huge integrity and
godliness, have run off after illicit sexual gratification, pride or

some weird doctrine, often wrecking many others' lives at the same time.

I don't believe that God means us to abandon all trust in people – that would be hellish and life simply wouldn't work. But too often we follow our own selfish ways, with the result that we need to know that we can put our full trust, finally, in God alone. And that he does watch over the innocent victims whose trust is betrayed. They may have to wait, but they need to know that Jesus' words (though in context they refer to children) aren't ageist:

> Whoever welcomes a little child like this in my name welcomes me. But if anyone causes one of these little ones who believe in me to sin, it would be better for him to have a large millstone hung around his neck and to be drowned in the depths of the sea.　　　　　　　　　　　　　　　　(Matthew 18.5–6)

Colin Raynor from Yorkshire was a social worker for over twenty-five years, specializing in work with foster carers and the children they tried to help. He often came across situations such as the one he describes here, of a mother talking with her daughter about her foster child and that child's father:

> 'She's breathing on the window and then writing her name. I get into trouble if I do that, don't I, Mum?'
>
> Her daughter's question could not be avoided. 'Yes. You are right. I don't like my windows messing up but Katy is anxious about her dad's visit, so I have to be a bit lenient with her. I'll have words with her later.'
>
> 'Will he come, Mum? He promised he would come last week and never turned up. If our dad says he's going to do something he . . .'
>
> 'Yes, well, we must be thankful that our dad is our dad, and we must also remember that Katy loves her dad, whatever we might think about him, just as much as you love your dad.'

'Where's her mum?'

'I'm not sure. I don't think her parents are together just now.' The foster mother gave a vague answer knowing she could never divulge the full details of why little Katy had to cling to faint hope of her father's visit in order to give her young life any meaning.

Suddenly there was a shout from the other room and Katy came charging through the kitchen to the front door.

'He's here. He's here. I knew he would come. I told you he would come.'

'Just a minute young lady. Don't forget your coat and that little parcel we wrapped up for your dad.'

But the foster mother's words were to no avail. Katy had flung open the door and thrown herself into the arms of the man who stood there.

Does he realize, thought the foster mother, just how special he is to that little girl and how he is her whole world? I do hope he does. Oh I do hope he does.

The passage from Micah goes on to say in verse 11: 'The day for building your walls will come.' Pray for all those who wait, only to be disappointed, that safe 'walls' of dependable trust might be restored. Pray especially for children and all who are especially vulnerable.

* * *

Thieves that ambush those who wait

The ground of a certain rich man produced a good crop. He thought to himself, 'What shall I do? I have no place to store my crops.'

Then he said, 'This is what I'll do. I will tear down my barns and build bigger ones, and there I will store all my grain and my goods. And I'll say to myself, "You have plenty of good things laid up for many years. Take life easy; eat, drink and be merry." '

But God said to him, 'You fool! This very night your life will be demanded from you. Then who will get what you have prepared for yourself?'

This is how it will be with anyone who stores up things for himself but is not rich towards God.   (Luke 12.16–21)

The man in Jesus' parable reminds me of King Solomon, who started out being greatly blessed. David had worked hard establishing the kingdom; now its riches were at Solomon's disposal. He started well, building the temple, asking for the gift of wisdom. But then, as with many who don't have to wait and work for good things, all veered awry. Power, wealth and women became his goals – whatever happened to the wisdom of a man who took 300 wives and 700 concubines? His sons turned out bad and from the glory days of God-fearing King David, the kingdom descended into a mess that lasted centuries, robbing its people of everything for which they had waited ever since the covenants with Abraham and Moses.

What thief lies in wait to ambush us as we wait? With the man in Jesus' story and with Solomon, it was hedonism – have a good time, don't bother about God or others. Eat, drink and be merry, for tomorrow you . . . oh yes – die. Die 'poor towards God'. There is always so much more on offer than simply having a good time. But there are worse 'thieves' lying in wait to rob us as we wait for the fullness of God's promise: cynicism, worry, fear, boredom, indolence – or simply lack of vision.

Debra Elsdon came on one of my writing holidays whose theme was 'Waves on Our Shore' and wrote a parable which she called 'Seaworthy':

Oh, it is a beautiful boat. Made with love and much care. The wood has been planed and shaped, sealed and painted. Its length is elegant and the tall mast dressed in the best sailcloth. Within the shell of the boat the wood is stained a delicate blue and the seats smoothed and so fashioned to afford comfort to any who would sit there.

It is a beautiful boat, all right – and in a brightly varnished trunk on board are charts and flares and instruments for measuring distance and angles and all that is required to navigate a steady course.

It is a beautiful boat and I sit in it nearly every day where it rests on its wooden supports. From there I can see the ocean, vast, twinkling, breakers frothing. It is a lovely view, a comfortable situation.

Still, I can't shake the feeling that something is missing.

On the same holiday, part-time scribe Noel Allsup wrote a more positive piece which he called 'From Shore to Sea':

I sensed that the water was cold. Self-preservation urged, 'Some other time' but the spirit of action argued, 'This opportunity will never be repeated.' The sea's darkness endorsed the first but the dancing, sparkling foam beckoned and won the second.

I took off my T-shirt and sandals slowly; not for me the headlong rush and heart-stopping plunge into permafrost! Wincing in anticipation, I stepped into the shallows – to my surprise, a wet, warm caress assured. I moved to receive a higher level as the tide came in, over knees, waist, circling chest – then the breakers claimed me. We danced together, waves and I, as they swept me towards the shore, as one in the flattening, spreading circle along the sand.

Shame tinged my delight; the brine could have been unbearable, but instead rewarded a spirit of adventure.

Life can be like that – fear of something non-existent. Even when an experience take us in its cold grip, at least we have proved something in adversity, to bless the days of imparted joy. And to the Christian, the Creator of the shores and seas promises: 'I am with you, always (Yes, even to the end of the age!)' (Matthew 28.20).

Help us not to wait and be robbed when we could be plunging into all that you have for us, Lord – when it's your time for us to bring blessing to others.

Talking of robbery, my friend Janet Catsaras had been through a particularly difficult time when she wrote the following poem on another writing holiday with the same 'Waves on Our Shore' theme. Neither of us knew she was about to endure far worse circumstances. Meanwhile she seized that holiday moment to write something which I think all of us could use as a defence against being robbed. Even during bleak, difficult periods of waiting we can find, or remember, some shafts of light and moments of calm. We may turn our backs and be robbed or choose to seek out good moments, embrace and enjoy them – and be strengthened.

Sometimes . . . just sometimes

Just sometimes
Stop
Swollering
And hollering
And wallowing.
Cease scratching at the sores.
Just sometimes
Skid and skate and snorkel at the shore.
Sing softly.

See the simmering, shimmering sunlight
Swathing the sandy seashore.
Sense the smiling, strongly scented sunshine
Smoothing and soothing.

Yes, rocks rise up rugged and steep
Sharply jagged, concealing the presence
Of deep, deep, dark waters
Hidden beneath.

But sometimes, just sometimes,
Sing softly, on the sandy seashore.

* * *

Weighted . . . or weighting?

You have been weighed on the scales and found wanting.
(Daniel 5.27)

During a period of waiting, have you ever felt that you've been weighed, found wanting and thrown on the scrap heap? That the reason why you're sidelined is that you're rubbish and this is God's judgement? I suspect many of us have found that 'thief' lying in ambush as we wait.

Of course, God does judge evil. Imagine the consequences if he didn't! In the story from Daniel, the king of Babylon, Belshazzar, who wanted for nothing and had been as all-powerful as his father, King Nebuchadnezzar, is 'weighed in the balance and found wanting'.

Belshazzar (in Daniel 5.23), is rebuked:

> . . . you have set yourself up against the LORD of heaven. You had the goblets from his temple brought to you, and you and your nobles, your wives and your concubines drank wine from them. You praised the gods of silver and gold, of bronze, iron, wood and stone, which cannot see or hear or understand. But you did not honour the God who holds in his hand your life and all your ways.

Nor did Belshazzar learn from the judgement God brought on his father who,

> when his heart became arrogant and hardened with pride . . . was deposed from his royal throne and stripped of his glory . . . driven away from people and given the mind of an animal . . . until he acknowledged that the Most High God is sovereign over the kingdoms of men and sets over them anyone he wishes.
>
> (Daniel 5.20–21)

Nebuchadnezzar repented; Belshazzar was slain that night and his kingdom given to Darius the Mede. And you? If you ever feel weighed down in your waiting, before you listen to any accusing voices inside your head that add to your misery, telling you that you're rubbish fit only for the scrap heap – consider whether or not you're a ruthless dictator over millions of miserable subjects. No? Well then, have you set yourself against God, doing your worst to provoke and anger him, desecrating all that is holy, becoming something demonic?

Have you any right even to think that you might be rubbish, when God created you and loves you? He knows you're not perfect, but he's invested a huge amount in you. Isn't this time of waiting more likely to be his making the odd adjustment or two as investments in you, rather than his last-resort judgement reserved for hardened long-term rebels?

Paula Felstead suffers from a number of ongoing health problems, including asthma. Not strong enough to pursue her career in the classroom she teaches dyslexic children on a one-to-one basis. She writes:

> I've been in a waiting situation for about six months now. I've had to move back to my parents' home because I couldn't find anywhere else that I could afford. I have also been unable

to find a new job that I'm strong enough to manage, yet will pay the bills. Furthermore, my father has cancer and we are waiting to see what the doctors can do for him. I admit I have spent much of the last six months seeing this as a very negative time; I assumed that I'd taken a wrong turning in my life and that's why all this had happened. I thought that it was probably my fault; after all, we are told that we reap what we sow. One word that kept coming into my mind was 'weighed' and the phrase from Daniel 5.26–28: '*Mene, mene, tekel, parsin*'; part of this translates as 'You have been weighed on the scales and found wanting.' But every time I asked God for direction so that I could move on from my past mistakes, he just seemed to say 'wait'. This felt like a literal weight on my mind!

Recently, though, I began to realize that I should make the most of this time. It is an opportunity to do things I am unable to do, normally. It's also an exciting time, like a pregnancy, when I know there will be changes ahead. It is a time to prepare, not by buying baby clothes or decorating a nursery, but by using my time wisely. Now every day brings new ideas and challenges.

Today, another version of being weighed came to mind, giving me a more positive outlook. The *Concise Oxford Dictionary* states that weighting is: 'extra . . . allowances given in special cases . . . e.g. to allow for the higher cost of living in London.' Now, I try not to get frustrated and agitated; instead, I tell myself that I am one of God's 'special cases' and that this time of waiting is his 'extra allowance' to me.

Paula wrote this poem about the paradoxical ups and downs of her life and relationship with God. Use it as a guide as you pray for those who wait – or as a hopeful meditation if you are yourself waiting.

Trust

The tide on the shore;
the stones and the sand;
being alone, but holding his hand.

An asthma attack,
fighting for breath;
a long life ahead, yet imminent death.

Active and passive;
busy and still;
creative ideas that conform to his will.

Dyslexic, confusing;
light comes and it goes;
but during the waiting, relationship grows.

Punctuates feeling;
searches for peace;
learns to relate and then to release.

The tide on the shore;
the stones and the sand;
being alone, yet holding his hand.

*   *   *

Waiting as *robbery: procrastination*

Elijah went before the people and said, 'How long will you waver
between two opinions? If the LORD is God, follow him; but if
Baal is God, follow him.' But the people said nothing.

(1 Kings 18.21)

The Bible contains many human cries, 'How long, Lord?' But
just as many times it's God who is crying, 'How long before my
people (or you) will . . . ?' Times when people waited, sitting

on the fence perhaps, when they should have acted or spoken up for what was right.

If there's 'a time to search and a time to give up, a time to keep and a time to throw away' (Ecclesiastes 3.6), there is a time to wait patiently and a time when you have to start moving, take action, do something.

Some of us are Simon Peter characters who leap impulsively into the water and act without thinking or hesitating. Others like to take a nice safe option, sticking with the crowd, avoiding making the difficult decision, let alone doing anything about it. Israel had become like that under the bad King Ahab and his wicked wife Jezebel – far too dangerous to speak up for God, let alone follow him, when the tyrants told them to worship Baal. It was only when Elijah demonstrated that God's power was greater than that of Baal and his priests, Ahab and Jezebel all put together that, 'the people fell prostrate and cried, "The Lord – he is God! The Lord – he is God!"'

Hesitate when you should be acting, let the would-be dictator get away with a few things and suddenly no one's life is worth living. Accept the status quo and there's nothing to wait for, nothing to look forward to, no chance of change for the better. You've been robbed!

Mary Hobbs told me an extraordinary story, but perhaps this kind of thing is, or was, not as uncommon as one might think.

My mother contracted multiple sclerosis soon after my birth, then went into remission, with certain restrictions and difficulties, until I was fourteen. Then Mum took a fall which left her shaken up. She had also contracted a urinary infection – recognized now to cause temporary confusion in MS patients. Mum didn't know night from day. Her memory vanished and confusion reigned.

The doctors decided that a suitable place for her would be a psychiatric hospital called Netherne and there she resided for six long years. Every Sunday Dad and I would catch the 472 bus to Coulsdon and trudge up the winding road to the top of the hill. I thought the grounds and the view beautiful – such a contrast with what we knew we would find inside the buildings.

Bags of goodies in hand, we would wait patiently for the locked doors of the ward to be opened. Inside, the other inmates sat around the walls in varying states of dress or undress, quietude or crazy murmurings. At least Mum had a room of her own for some of the time and there she would be sitting, as ever, patiently waiting for us. Dad would produce a flask and home-made Victoria sponge and we would proceed to have tea together. It must have been the highlight of her week. Each time she would ask, 'When am I coming home?' but Netherne had become the norm now and her question remained unanswered for those six long years.

To me, things seemed normal enough, though I grew up too fast. My week consisted of school, sharing the chores with Dad and much-needed time with close friends and relatives. I left school after O levels and entered the Civil Service. About the time I reached the age of twenty it dawned on me that Mum had been steadily improving over the years. Why was she still in Netherne? Dad seemed content with life as it was. I realized that, if anything were to change, I must be the catalyst.

Given some gentle pressure, my dad approached the authorities, and soon we were bringing Mum home for week-ends – how hard to take her back to Netherne afterwards! Next she moved to a convalescent hospital closer to home. Finally, by the time of my twenty-first birthday, Mum was living with us again, the locked doors of Netherne a thing of the past, though she had not 'recovered' from her incapacity and needed constant help and care, not least with her physical toiletries. From the time of her return home until her death some fourteen years later – by which time I was married with a growing family – my father ministered tenderly and uncomplainingly to her every need.

Mary says she does understand now why her father took no action all those years – he had issues of his own. But how each member of that family was robbed, not only by multiple sclerosis, but by that prolonged interlude at Netherne!

Lord, it's not always easy to know when to act and when to wait. Show us! We pray particularly for people who can't make those decisions for themselves, because they are too young or have mental health problems perhaps. Especially show us when and how to take effective action on behalf of those who can't free themselves from oppression, injustice or suffering.

* * *

Waiting as *robbery – pre-emption*

'This is my covenant with you: You will be the father of many nations . . . I will make you very fruitful; I will make nations of you, and kings will come from you . . . As for . . . your wife . . . I will bless her and will surely give you a son by her. I will bless her so that she will be the mother of nations; kings of peoples will come from her.'

Abraham fell face down; he laughed and said to himself, 'Will a son be born to a man a hundred years old? Will Sarah bear a child at the age of ninety?'

And Abraham said to God, 'If only Ishmael might live under your blessing!'   (Genesis 17.4–6, 15–18)

If we've been promised something which doesn't materialize, it's so easy to become impatient and snatch, though we may half-destroy it in the process. That's what Abraham and his wife did when they had been in Canaan for ten long years, growing older without any sign of the son God had promised them.

There were bitter consequences. Abraham's wife mistreated her pregnant maidservant, who fled. The angel of the Lord rescued this Hagar in the desert. Before sending her back to Abraham, he said that her son would be, 'A wild donkey of a man; his hand will be against everyone and everyone's hand against him, and he will live in hostility towards all his brothers' (Genesis 16.12).

Yet all was not lost. Abraham's son by Hagar the maidservant was born and named 'Ishmael', meaning 'God listens'. Thirteen years later, God appeared and promised Abraham another son, by Sarah his wife, in the words quoted above. He also said,

> And as for Ishmael, I have heard you: I will surely bless him; I will make him fruitful and will greatly increase his numbers. He will be the father of twelve rulers, and I will make him into a great nation. But my covenant I will establish with Isaac, whom Sarah will bear to you by this time next year.
>
> (Genesis 17.20–21)

We can jump the gun, stepping outside of God's will – that carries consequences. But God's redemptive grace has a habit of breaking through to win the day. Someone once pictured it as God drawing his plans like circles. Human beings break and destroy a circle but God simply draws a larger circle around it, encompassing the old plans and making them bigger.

Jane Terry writes of something which happened within her family:

> When we had been married a few months my husband and I decided that we could just afford to start a family. I wasn't earning very much, so the lack of my wages wouldn't be too great a loss. I loved children and intended to stay at home and

be a full-time mother. We worked things out and even decided the time of year that the baby should be born.

So I was rather taken aback when nothing happened and, as month after month went by, I became more and more depressed. For several years we went through the performance of temperature charts – was there really supposed to be some pattern in the squiggles that emerged? Trips to the doctor and the hospital were all to no avail. This was before the time of IVF.

I thought that perhaps if I prayed God would give me a baby, but no, he didn't seem to be listening. Then I grew angry with him. Didn't I have as much right to a baby as the next person? (I learned later that we have no rights – anything good is a gift.) I cried, 'If you're not going to let me have a baby, God, then you shouldn't have made me fond of them in the first place!'

I decided to take matters into my own hands and adopt a baby. Now that is a lovely thing to be able to do, but my attitude was all wrong. However, years ago there were many more babies available for adoption than there are today, so we were interviewed and visited and in due course were given a lovely baby boy. A few years later we adopted a sister for him.

So we lived happily ever after? I'm afraid not. Although the children were well and happy the anger I had felt had caused a rift between God and me. Our relationship wasn't nearly as good.

Only when I began to want to put God first in my life, some years later, did I see how self-willed I had been. I remembered some people in the Bible who had done much the same thing as I had. Abraham and Sarah, too impatient to wait for the son God had promised them, opted for a surrogate mother, using their maid to give them a son.

I was very sorry when I recognized myself in the story of their lives, but I know that God forgave me as he did them. So were they wasted years? No, I don't think so. Who knows, perhaps God might have wanted us to adopt children anyway.

Whatever the original plan, it is good to realize that God still loves our family and wants the best for us. But life is certainly happier doing things with him than without him.

Lord, so often we're robbed because we try to do things in our way and according to our timing without waiting for you. You're God – it is right that we fit in with you and absurd that we should ever think it should be the other way around. We're sorry, Lord – and we thank you for your grace which so often restores what our impatient haste has damaged.

Waiting on *or* at . . .

Waiting on the edge of a cliff, of a crowd, on the shores of loneliness and longing, at a crossroads . . . or waiting on God? I wrote
the following poem after reading a book about Genesis by Trevor
Dennis (*Looking God in the Eye*, SPCK, 1998). It pointed out
that Jacob's significant encounters with God (the ladder, the
wrestling with the angel of the Lord and so on) all occurred
when he was at the edge of the land promised to his people.
When I've felt dangerously pushed out to the edge, waiting there
uncomfortably, those times have often become a well of creativity and spiritual growth.

Apparent contradictions or 'paradoxes' aren't easy to express
or to understand, yet seem to lie at the heart of our faith,
especially when we're waiting . . .

On the edge

Here, on the buffeted boundary between
poetry and prose, prophecy
and imagination, what is . . . is not . . . may be,
we see needs, resources, the broken ladder
between.
Few fences prevent faith pushing
unexplored territory too far.
Roads snake back before
reaching this place where our fire, lit for warmth
and safety, wind-whipped, may burn disaster.

Good is not evil but we carry both within
to edges of sheer fall, to brimming rivers

that require dry miracles to cross.
We've built our cairns,
pillowed a holy place, been not always lonely –
yet still rely on our defences,
forgetting death exists in birth, sleep, love
(but, strangely, not eternity).

So, tripping paradox wires
set at the growing edges of your kingdom,
we learn to live upside down, on our faces, on our knees.

Waiting on . . . *the edge*

When I was a child, I talked like a child, I thought like a child,
I reasoned like a child. When I became a man, I put childish
ways behind me. Now we see but a poor reflection as in a
mirror; then we shall see face to face. Now I know in part; then
I shall know fully, even as I am fully known.

(1 Corinthians 13.11–12)

I suppose all Christians, in a sense, are waiting on the edge, waiting in the uncomfortable borderlands between time and eternity. We've entered God's kingdom that hasn't fully come yet,
not on earth. We know God . . . in part. We are being saved.
Healed, we're not yet whole. There's a whole lot more to come.
We wait, in faith, in hope, in love . . .

Some people, often because of their experience of far-from-
perfect human relationships, find it especially hard to feel close
to God the Father. Marjorie Kiddle writes here of her long wait
on the edge of knowing the Father – and of how it came to an
end as she grew to understand better Jesus' relationship with
him. I've known Marjorie for a few years now and though in
her eighties and in a lot of pain, I would say that over those
years she has grown tremendously in confidence and joy. So it

was worth the wait – she may be small and frail now, but positively glows with the Spirit of God within her.

Before my twin sister and I reached our third birthday, sadly our parents had died. Our sister aged seven and brother aged eleven completed our little family. Our dear maternal granny came to the rescue and could not have been a more wonderful, loving and caring mother-substitute. Her sister, Great-Auntie Maggie, came alongside to share the task of caring for us, her long experience as a children's nanny proving absolutely invaluable. Pennies were short in our home, and had to be carefully managed, but love was in abundant supply, from both Granny and Auntie. Our father and mother were of course irreplaceable, and as we grew up there were inevitably some gaps in our family experiences.

In my mid-twenties I experienced the joy of knowing Jesus as Saviour. No doubt because of my childhood bereavement, I did not relate to God as my heavenly Father in a meaningful way. Although of course in my head I knew it to be true, I longed for this to be an experience of my heart.

As I have reread the Gospels in recent days, I have become very aware of the intimate relationship Jesus had with his Father when he was on earth. At his visit to the temple when he was twelve years old (Luke 2.41–52) Jesus spoke of his desire to be in his Father's house and to be about his business. He heard the wonderful affirmation of his Father's love at his baptism in the Jordan: 'This is my son whom I love' (Matthew 3:17). I discovered that on almost every page of John's Gospel Jesus is recorded as talking to, or about, his Father, and his oneness with him.

The record of Jesus telling his disciples of his Father's love for them was particularly telling. One verse spoke especially to me. In John 16.27a (translation *God's New Covenant*, by Heinz Cassirer, Eerdmans, 1989), Jesus is recorded as saying, 'The Father himself holds you dear because of your holding me dear.' My waiting was over! I had no doubt of the reality of my heavenly Father's love for me. Of course, I had read these passages many times, but the Holy Spirit spoke to me through them in a new and living way. I read again the story of the resurrection and Jesus' words to Mary Magdalene, 'I am returning to my Father, and your Father, to my God and your God' (John 20.17) – another affirmation!

My waiting was at an end; I was eighty-two years old – but thank God he has a heavenly calendar!

Thank you, Lord that we might feel as though we're waiting on the edge, or even falling off it – but you have no edges or borders. We may not know you as fully as we might, yet you know us – and somehow love us too!

> O LORD, you have searched me and you know me.
> You know when I sit and when I rise; you perceive my thoughts from afar.
> You discern my going out and my lying down; you are familiar with all my ways.
> Before a word is on my tongue you know it completely, O LORD.
> You hem me in – behind and before; you have laid your hand upon me.
> Such knowledge is too wonderful for me, too lofty for me to attain.
> Where can I go from your Spirit? Where can I flee from your presence?
> If I go up to the heavens, you are there; if I make my bed in the depths, you are there.
> If I rise on the wings of the dawn, if I settle on the far side of the sea,
> even there your hand will guide me, your right hand will hold me fast.

(Psalm 139.1–10)

* * *

Waiting on . . . *the edge – old age*

Since my youth, O God, you have taught me, and to this day
I declare your marvellous deeds. Even when I am old and grey,
do not forsake me, O God, till I declare your power to the next
generation, your might to all who are to come . . . Though you
have made me see troubles, many and bitter, you will restore
my life again; from the depths of the earth you will again bring
me up. You will increase my honour and comfort me once again.

(Psalm 71.17–21)

My parents live in a pleasant retirement village, which its residents jokingly dub 'The Waiting Room'. The bitter 'enemies'
of cancer and heart disease, dementia and arthritis stalk
through its bungalows, proving the residents' adage that, 'It's
not much fun growing old – but the alternative's no better!'
Of course, Christians can look forward to heaven, but suppose
your beloved spouse dies before you do? And isn't it sad, watching all these people who once did exciting, significant things,
slowly robbed of their faculties, becoming 'practically useless'
as they wait to die?

That's one way of looking at it. Another is that many of these
people have proved God's care for them over a lifetime. He's
worked with them in helping others and they have amazing
stories to tell. Some individuals, conscious now of their own
mortality, turn to him for the first time in their lives.

Nevertheless it's still not much fun growing old, and with
life expectancy increasing year on year, most of us will spend
more time than previous generations did in the 'waiting room'.
How might we best approach this? Maybe we can learn from
the psalmist who appeared to be on the edge, almost beyond
hope. Earlier he had written (verses 9–10), 'Do not cast me away
when I am old; do not forsake me when my strength is gone.
For my enemies speak against me; those who wait to kill me

conspire together.' Yet he rehearses all the good things God has done and doesn't lose hope.

Lewis Wallace came on one of my writing holidays, contributing much in the way of laughter, creativity and wisdom. As I waved him off at the end of our time together I thought how remarkable this man in his eighties was to drive hundreds of miles back home on his own. He had insisted on carrying his own small bag to the car and I admired the way he could travel so light. Then he wrote his story for me – and I wondered even more at his courage and God's faithfulness.

The separation from my wife was a last act of despair on both our parts. For four years her deteriorating mental condition had put such a strain on our relationship that staying together would be too dangerous. My constant desperate prayers seemed unavailing and only the help of a therapist saved me from having a severe nervous breakdown.

Our elder daughter soon found a flat for each of us near her own home fifty miles away. Yet as I started to leave church at the end of my first Sunday service in the new town, I still felt utterly vulnerable until a much younger lady suddenly stepped into the aisle and gave me a warm, comforting hug. One which had me feeling as if I were the original prodigal son returning home.

It was a good sign. Soon I found myself playing the organ at one or other of the associated churches. Then after one service the preacher beckoned me aside to say, 'You know, God sent you here' – which would have been encouraging had God shown any interest when my need was greatest. Or so I thought at the time. Yet that preacher's words kept nagging at me until I started going over all that had happened.

There had been a commonsense reason behind my move there, while the hug had seemed mere happenstance – even if it was the reason that I joined that young lady's church home group where I found friendship, an understanding of my needs and very real support in my difficulties. But above all there had been one other thing. Ever since the move, I'd known I still needed expert constant help to get me on my feet again, so I had phoned my previous therapist to ask if there was anyone she could recommend. Incredibly she told me that she also had a practice near my flat . . . the only professional covering both areas.

That was one coincidence too many to take at face value. Which was why, after the next home group meeting, I asked the lady concerned what had led her to give me that hug – and got the answer, 'I don't know. I just suddenly felt I had to.'

That night my prayers were very humble and next day I started writing a psalm of thanksgiving. Not that all my prayers or questions have been answered. After a massive stroke, my wife is now virtually disabled, confined to her living room and bedroom, seeing only her carers and myself, plus our daughters when their work permits. Yet all trace of that mental illness has disappeared. Last year we celebrated our golden wedding anniversary with all nine of our family around the festive table.

Lewis found it helpful to write his own psalm. Maybe you could write yours? Or pray his yourself, for someone known to you who endures the long wait (and weight) of caring, or for someone who struggles with despair in old age.

> O Lord my God
> Your mercies abound throughout all the world, and your
>   loving kindness extends to all men.
>
> When my troubles came upon me, I said, Where is my God?
>   Where is he who promised that his angels would lift me up
>   in their hands lest I dash my foot against a stone?
>
> I called to you, but heard no answer. I cried from the depths
>   of my being, but there was no reply.

Yet little by little I was lifted up. Day by day the steep and
  stony path became smoother, until my soul cried out,
  'The Lord has been with you. His spirit has dwelt within
  you, guiding you to green pastures.'

Therefore, O Lord, will I praise you day by day. Your presence
  will be extolled by me throughout the night watches.

O God my God,
truly it is said how manifold are your mercies throughout all
  the world, and how infinite your loving kindness to all who
  call upon you.

*   *   *

Waiting at . . . *the crossroads*

Going a little farther, he fell with his face to the ground and
prayed, 'My Father, if it is possible, may this cup be taken from
me. Yet not as I will, but as you will.'
  Then he returned to his disciples and found them sleeping.
'Could you men not keep watch with me for one hour?' he asked
Peter.
  'Watch and pray so that you will not fall into temptation.
The spirit is willing, but the body is weak.'

(Matthew 26.39–41)

Waiting must have been appalling for Jesus, knowing his time
to be crucified was nearly upon him and that his closest
friends still didn't understand. He realized that the hours and
days to come would be incredibly hard for them too – that's
partly why he prayed for them in advance. He started that prayer:
'Father, the time has come. Glorify your Son, that your Son may
glorify you' (John 17.1). Yes, the agony would be beyond im-
agining but through it his disciples and so many more would
come into a glorious relationship with his Father. He had faith

that his struggling disciples would emerge from those dark days of his crucifixion and burial, to enter a life of eternal quality. He had faith that they would continue his work and that the Father would continue to keep them from evil. 'My prayer is not for them alone. I pray also for those who will believe in me through their message' (John 17.20).

Still, that hour in Gethsemane must have been the longest short wait for Jesus. He could have refused the 'cup'. He could have chosen to leave Jerusalem, escape to safety, avoid the cross.

When we wait at any crossroads, the easiest way doesn't necessarily lead to the best future – for us and/or others. The horribly hard way might. Are we desperate enough to follow the narrow and difficult way of the cross? If we do, we are not alone, there is help.

Tom Wettern works for a leading UK rehabilitation centre which delivers groundbreaking treatment for drug and alcohol addiction. He writes about 'The Longest Short Wait':

> Addiction to drugs forces a person to travel a rocky path. At first the road seems full of liberating possibilities but, as they prove illusory, the journey becomes wearisome. Old baggage weighs ever more heavily. In the destructive abyss, amid the ongoing agony of waiting for fleeting gratification, buried feelings surface – shame, fear, self-hate, churning guilt . . . Occasionally a distant hope flickers in the swirling drug-fuelled maelstrom – could recovery be a possibility?
>
> But any recovery is a journey, not an event. Each day – each minute within it, a blessing never taken for granted – will involve pain, anger, sadness and fear. As there is never a cure, there's nothing to wait for. Yet there will be hope and the chance to learn self-love, to live life in the present with the help of growing inner resources and the love of those who stay close. Live each day, a day at a time. Each day is a day in recovery.

But first there is the last wait, to be accepted into rehab . . .

'You really want this?' asked the doctor at the rehab centre.

'Desperately,' pleaded the addict, unable to inject the passion he wanted into his response. A life of trickery and deception had leached the capacity for feelings from him.

'How do I know you'll see it through?'

'This is the chance, my last chance.'

'Go on.'

The addict detected a flash of mistrust in the doctor's granite demeanour. 'That's it. No more to it. This is the time. I'm at the bottom. Tried before and bombed out. Have to grasp the rope and not let go.'

He was shaking. Withdrawal had started to set in. No fix for what seemed like days, even years, but in fact was only a matter of hours. He couldn't remember when he'd last gone that long. What if this man didn't believe him? He knew what he'd do if he were turned away. Even as the doctor's stare drained his optimism he thought – *I could walk out now . . . No I wouldn't . . . I . . .*

'Would you like some water?' the doctor asked.

Water godammit. Bastard. Let me in or let me get out of here, now. The demons of withdrawal rattled the gates of his crumbling resolve. *Please . . . just say the word.*

'Thank you, I'm fine, really. I just don't feel that good. I . . .'

'It's OK. I've been there too. It does get better. But we have to know you'll stay the course, not just for you, but for the sake of others who are recovering here.'

Sod the others. It's about me. What I want. What I want now.

'I will. I'm committed. Anything you ask. I'll do it. Please . . .'

Look inside. See the determination glimmering in my darkness. Believe me. Go on.

'Please!' he sobbed.

There was a knock at the door.

106

'Come. Ben. Hi. Come in.'

Serenity exuded from the lanky arrival.

'This is Ben. He'll be your buddy. That means he'll look after you, show you the ropes. He's been through it too, like you and I.'

However extreme the consequences of crossroads – and the first and then moment-by-moment decisions to stay clear of hard drugs must be huge – Jesus has been through worse. In Tom's story, the doctor and Ben asked the addict to walk only where they had walked, and it is the same with Jesus. That gives us hope as we wait for a pain-filled path to lead us to a better place.

He understands and somehow walks alongside as well as in front. Psalm 16.8 says: 'I have set the LORD always before me. Because he is at my right hand, I shall not be shaken.' Meditate on this as you pray for yourself or others who wait now at crossroads or who wait for difficult roads to become less of a struggle.

* * *

Waiting on . . . *the edge of life and death*

Yet the LORD longs to be gracious to you; he rises to show you compassion. For the LORD is a God of justice. Blessed are all who wait for him! O people of Zion, who live in Jerusalem, you will weep no more. How gracious he will be when you cry for help! As soon as he hears, he will answer you. Although the Lord gives you the bread of adversity and the water of affliction, your teachers will be hidden no more; with your own eyes you will see them. Whether you turn to the right or to the left, your ears will hear a voice behind you, saying, 'This is the way; walk in it.'   (Isaiah 30.18–21)

It doesn't feel very 'blessed' to be waiting at the edges of life, be it birth or death. I remember the wait for my first baby – due on 10 December. 'Still here?' my friends would chorus, laughing, when I confounded all expectations by showing up at endless pre-Christmas celebrations.

I never imagined still being in hospital at New Year. My new baby's skin had turned as yellow as that of the lovely Malaysian sister in charge of the ward, while doctors muttered dark warnings of risks associated with the exchange transfusion which our blood incompatibility might make necessary.

'As soon as he hears, he will answer you'? Well, perhaps. Certainly it didn't feel 'soon' at the time but after specific prayer my baby's condition did improve 'on its own' in early January. Finally we returned home.

When waiting for something as momentous as birth, or death, God's 'soon' is our long-drawn-out agony. To us 'a matter of life or death' implies urgency, yet from the point of view of life eternal, of God, there is no real 'edge', no great divide. Those in a living relationship with him can be born anew every morning into a freshness of faith and wonder.

I remember the hospital calling us to my father-in-law's bedside. 'He's deteriorated rapidly during the night and might not last until visiting time this afternoon.' As he lay there, unconscious, we listened for several hours to his laboured breathing. Nothing appeared to change. There was so little that we or the hospital could do. The next few days, waiting for him to die, seemed cruel. Job said: 'In his hand is the life of every creature and the breath of all mankind' (12.10). That's comforting but also accusatory. If every breath is in God's hands, why does he prolong the agony?

How do we walk these or far worse 'edges' without falling down precipitous cliffs to the left or slipping into the slimy swamp on our right? How do we eat the 'bread of adversity' and drink the 'water of affliction', yet prevent the poison of bitterness from entering our guts? Can we keep faith with a 'gracious, compassionate' God, the good 'Teacher' who shows us each step of the way? Can we believe, however close we feel to falling off the edge of faith ourselves, that he will hold us, giving the strength we need to support others?

The Revd Ruth Walker from Surrey wrote with great honesty about waiting for her elderly mother to die:

> How much longer, Lord?
> How many times did I utter those words?
> How much longer must I watch my mum slowly slipping out
> of the tiny shell that was her body?
> The once indomitable wee Scot, now reduced to a confused,
> mumbling little old lady.
> How much longer must I watch my dad – her devoted
> husband of sixty years – make the twice-daily journey
> to hold her hand, to force spoonfuls of food through
> shrivelled lips?
> How many more admissions to hospital. 'She may not last
> the night' – only to rally yet again?
> And the agony goes on.
> The agony of remembering being enfolded by a snuggly
> body – now a wasted shell.
> The agony of remembering her singing, 'I'd rather have Jesus.'
> Does she even know who he is now?
> How much longer?
> How much longer must I feel the guilt of uttering those
> words?
>
> Have you got the celestial Hoover out – making sure
> everything's as 'spick and span' as she always kept her
> home? Really, it doesn't matter.

You'll love having her there – why wait?

She'll be right in there – in the celestial kitchens – making the meringues and cream sponges for which she was so famous.

She'll be cuddling all the babies – she was always so snuggly.

She'll be picking out the right 'royal robes' for the newcomers – she always had a knack for that.

She'll be singing again – always such a big part of her life.

But, most importantly – she'll be Mum again.

Thank you, Father, that over the edge which we perceive, there is no more weeping, pain, decay or death. There Jesus – healer, redeemer, Saviour – reigns. All the light of life shines from him brighter than the sun. Give all who wait, for birth or death, a glimpse of that brilliance – informing a real hope, trust and strength here on earth.

Waiting on God

Holy Spirit

We cannot hold him in our hands –
his wind, his breath would rush away.
His flame is living, hot to burn.
His dove has bones that we might break,
wild wings that need to fly.
But we can welcome him –
the wind, the fire, the dove – and so
breathe life in us, Spirit, inspire,
then, breeze or whirlwind, send us forth;
warm us with fire, consume our dross,
touch our lips and bid us go;
then shelter us beneath dove's wing,
the soft, bright pillow of your breast,
flutter our hearts with love for you
and speak your words of ownership.
Draw alongside, Comforter,
and cup us in *your* hand.

* * *

God waits for us to change our attitude

The acts of the sinful nature are obvious . . . hatred, discord, jealousy, fits of rage, selfish ambition, dissensions, factions and envy . . . I warn you, as I did before, that those who live like this will not inherit the kingdom of God. But the fruit of the Spirit is love, joy, peace, patience, kindness, goodness, faithfulness, gentleness and self-control. Against such things there is no law . . . Since we live by the Spirit, let us keep in step with the Spirit.   (Galatians 5.19–25)

We may complain about waiting for God to do something but the Bible says just as much about his waiting for us. He waits patiently for us to grow into our inheritance, so that when we get to heaven, we'll enjoy it. God's a realist and knows that won't happen overnight. Maybe we avoid the grosser sexual sins that I've left out of the Scripture quote above. They tend to receive all the attention but, 'I've never been drunk in an orgy, aren't I good?' won't cut much ice with God! Christians can be jealous and selfish, we can fly off the handle, have pointless arguments, gossip or form cliques just as much as the next person. And exactly like the next person, the more we're told not to do something, the more attractive it can seem.

We know we 'shouldn't' do these things as Christians; we know we won't be displaying Christ-like attitudes or following our Lord if we do – but laws and 'shouldn'ts' don't help. It's fruit we need and fruit takes time to grow. It needs all the nourishment the tree (or the Spirit, sun and Son) can give. Likewise, learning to walk in step with the Spirit, or Jesus, takes time. It's counter-cultural, even counter-intuitive.

We recognize the fruit of the Spirit in people's lives, giving a little foretaste of what heaven might be like. If everyone is loving, peaceful and full of joy there, I wonder if we'll need patience? We certainly shall while living on earth as citizens of this kingdom of God which has arrived and yet, frustratingly, has not come fully. Maybe patience is one of the things which, as the children's carol 'Away in a manger' says, 'fit us for heaven' – the equivalent of one of those trace elements a plant needs in order for its fruit to grow as perfect and delicious as possible.

Rachel Kamara is a Methodist local preacher and circuit steward from West London. She comes from Sierra Leone and in *Leaning Towards Easter* (SPCK, 2005) I wrote about how, during the terrible troubles there, she sang praise to God while in prison. Released, she found the family house ransacked and all their possessions gone; then her husband was executed despite being found guilty of no crime. Meanwhile her daughter's husband in England died suddenly of a brain haemorrhage.

I know of Rachel through a friend who puts the highest value on a weekly prayer-time with her and says she – and the whole church – always learn so much from her. Yet here Rachel writes of a recent difficult experience of waiting which has helped her 'grow'.

I came to England to attend the funeral of my son-in-law after my husband was killed in Sierra Leone. It turned out that my daughter, who works for the NHS, needed help with her two boys aged five and two. They missed their father badly and, since the death of both of our husbands, my daughter was the sole breadwinner for them, herself and me. I applied to stay in this country to look after the boys and was given a one-year permit. As the end of this period drew near I called my solicitor for advice, and he submitted an application on my behalf for an extension.

My friends were always asking if there was any progress on my application. In a way this made matters worse, because every time it was mentioned, I'd be reminded of the problem and become worried all over again. It was a very anxious time. What would happen to me if I were sent back? Waiting was not easy especially since I had waited for my husband to come out of prison, only to find out that he was killed at the end.

The days went by so quickly and the time was almost up when my solicitor called me into the office and showed me a letter from the Home Office informing me that my application was rejected. However, if I thought this decision was not right, I could appeal. Immediately an application was sent off on my behalf. That gave me some peace of mind. I settled down to wait as best as I could. I could do nothing else.

After several weeks a letter informed me of the date of the appeal. I dreamt frequently about the hearing beforehand, only to find out in the morning that it had been a dream. With just two days to go, I took a trip to the court since I did not know how to get there. Then my solicitor informed me that the judge needed my daughter to attend, and so in the end she drove me there. A man and one lady were called in to cases before ours. Then I went in with my daughter and the barrister who was representing me. While waiting, all three of us prayed that God's will would be done.

I was expecting a very difficult hearing but my nerves calmed down as the judge and the representative from the Home Office put questions to me. Finally my daughter was called to testify that the accounts I had given were correct. We heard that we would receive word from the judge in a couple of weeks' time.

The waiting continued but in less than three weeks I received a letter requesting me to send a current passport to the Home Office as my present one had expired. I knew then that the waiting was worth it and that all had worked out well. I was given an extension of two years.

I learned at the time that in all you do – as long as you are honest and truthful – the Lord's will becomes evident, to give what is best for you. Since then I have learned to say, 'It was not meant to be'; instead of being anxious and worried all the time, I would ask that God's will be done. Worrying is not good for one's health and state of mind.

> Selfish ambition comes to nothing – a fruit grown too fast, blackened by frost.
> Trampling over others wrecks and squashes: peace, patience and gentleness restore.

Hatred destroys: kindness soothes and builds.
Worry withers: prayer and trust plumps us up with God's
goodness.
Envy embitters: loving service sweetens us – so that many can
feed and be thankful.

Thank you, Lord, that you are patient and good – that while we
stew about waiting for you, in reality you are waiting for us!

* * *

Waiting on God while he hides

Your face, Lord, I will seek. Do not hide your face from me,
do not turn your servant away in anger; you have been my helper.
Do not reject me or forsake me, O God my Saviour . . .
  I am still confident of this: I will see the goodness of the Lord
in the land of the living. Wait for the Lord; be strong and take
heart and wait for the Lord.   (Psalm 27.8–9, 13–14)

When we're waiting and nothing seems to happen, if only
we could see God's face, if only we could touch him. If only he
didn't appear to go away sometimes, to hide – especially in 'the
day of trouble'. He hides, we seek – or so the psalmist said. Why?
God's idea of a game or some cruel test? Surely not! Maybe it's
that something good starts to grow within us as we learn not
to seek his hand, primarily. Hands bring gifts, which may make
us greedy – or punishment, which may make us afraid. It's best
that such fruit doesn't grow at the core of our relationship with
him. Can we instead seek his face – his expression of love or
warning – searching out what he is, rather than what we can
get from him, drawing strength from that?
  Waiting, especially when his face remains hidden from our
view, requires strength and courage. The psalmist found those

things by reminding himself of the good things God had done in the past, by keeping a watch on his own thoughts and by choosing to declare positive ones. If you're a natural pessimist as I am, there are a few 'growing points' here. Even on a purely human level, when feeling misery, worry or despair, so much is in our attitude. Daft I know, but I find a smile helps, forcing it if necessary before discovering a real smile at my own 'Eeyore' tendencies. Surely life goes better for those who declare, 'It'll be all right on the night' than for those who mutter constantly about doom and disaster.

The psalmist did more than this though. He spoke to himself, to his own spirit, or directly to his will, perhaps. He set his priorities, centred around his relationship with God.

> One thing I ask of the LORD, this is what I seek: that I may dwell in the house of the LORD all the days of my life, to gaze upon the beauty of the LORD and to seek him in his temple. For in the day of trouble he will keep me safe in his dwelling; he will hide me in the shelter of his tabernacle and set me high upon a rock. (Psalm 27.4–5)

Ah, so now the psalmist is hidden *with* God, safe in his house!

Dorothy Gardiner, a Methodist lay preacher from Penarth, wrote this:

> I don't like to be kept waiting! Who does? But there's one person I'm happy to wait for – the Lord. When he says he will do something – I believe him. But oh, you have to have patience.
>
> Twenty years ago I became a Christian and started talking to the Lord. So imagine my surprise when just six weeks into our new relationship, he spoke to me as I offered up concern for my teenage daughter – you will know what I mean. His answer was immediate, unequivocal, overwhelming. 'I hear you. Be in peace, all is well.' His presence was so strong, so direct, that it

pinned me to my chair. I couldn't move for the peace and it seemed that from that moment on, all would be well.

But no – now, in her late thirties, she is a single mum with health problems including degenerative arthritis of the spine. She has three children, two of whom also have health problems which will become more apparent with age. I needed his precious gift of peace.

Then last month we visited Durham Cathedral. My husband and I spent the whole day exploring the height and depth and length and breadth of the presence of God in that beautiful place.

I discovered our daughter's birthday fell on St Cuthbert's saint's day. He is buried there and I spent some time in his shrine, praying for her – everything I could think of. I sealed my prayers by lighting a candle.

Back in our hotel I settled down to read the daily Scripture in our unopened newspaper. It was taken from Psalm 18: 'For you will light my candle. The Lord my God will lighten my darkness.' I slept well that night.

Next morning we returned for the Trinity Sunday communion – a service I believe holds his healing power and, as I hadn't prayed specifically for my daughter's back the previous day, that was my prayer offering.

We went forward for communion with the clergy ministering in twos so that you received from someone coming at a distance of two people away. It was the lovely woman who had taken the service who served me with the bread and as she came towards me, I found myself falling backwards. With nothing to hold on to it was difficult not to lose my balance.

I thought at first it was just this Spirit-filled woman. Then I thought, no, it's the power that's in that tiny host – the healing love of Christ given for us on the cross that we might know his risen life in our own, fallen lives.

Our daughter still has her bad back. Our grandchildren continue to suffer with their health problems. But God has said he will lighten the darkness and he has demonstrated the life that is to be had in the bread and the wine. I feed on those words every day and I eat his bread with renewed faith. They fill me, they satisfy me.

Only he knows the day and the hour of his coming into their lives. I will wait.

Lighten our darkness, Lord, hide us in your house, draw us close to your heart as we wait.

*   *   *

Waiting on God – seeing the bigger picture, from his perspective

Cast your bread upon the waters, for after many days you will find it again.   (Ecclesiastes 11.1)

The ancient wisdom contained in Ecclesiastes 11.1 speaks of a kind of investment very different from that undertaken by venture capitalists because, at its core, giving is more important than yield. 'Casting' or 'throwing' bread is rather more active than the modern version: 'What goes around, comes around.' All investments have one thing in common though – waiting. There may well be a long wait before people can look back and say, 'That worked' – and even longer to be able to say, for sure, 'That didn't work; all is lost!'

We've looked already at 'waiting as investment' – especially God's investment in us. You and I are important to him as individuals – but it's bigger than that. His investment in any one of us may end up helping who knows how many other people. From his perspective, each of us has a small but important part in *his*-story.

Here's one small example. Artist Jan Berry came on two of my writing holidays. Later, while I was undergoing tests and awaiting an operation for what turned out to be early-stage cancer, she sent me a beautiful card which she had painted, along with a poem she had written. That poem helped me perhaps more than anything else at that time because of its honesty and compassion – lines such as, 'Take my imagination that would rob/my days of hopeful joy' . . . My imagination had been working overtime – and not helpfully! Jan's poem moved me and reminded me that others struggled with the same things. It helped me grasp, in reality rather than theory, that God could take the rubbish I handed to him and turn it to good. Even if my imagination wasn't up to seeing how this might happen at the time. Even if I continued to struggle, rather than overflowing with joy and peace like a 'good Christian'. God is, after all, considerably bigger, wiser and more powerful than we are and has all the time in the world. So relying on him is wise, whatever the outcome, whatever the future.

When I asked if I might use her poem in this book, Jan agreed readily. She also sent the story of how she came to write it and what has happened since.

Heather was practice nurse at our local health centre as well as a friend from church. One sunny morning in 1993 she confided to me that she had found telltale signs of a health problem, which dampened our spirits as we talked together.

When it became clear that this was serious, I wrote a poem for her, entitled 'Awaiting the Diagnosis'. After six months of stringent tests and decreasing health, doctors and consultants failed to come up with anything they could identify. The symptoms increased and Heather grew weaker. Fearing we would lose her, we covered her with prayer. Then the breakthrough came. A doctor, new to the case, diagnosed non-Hodgkin's lymphoma. Miraculously, localized inflammation had stopped it spreading. The treatment was long and intensive; by God's grace she recovered and is still serving the Lord.

Seven years later I had cause to visit Heather professionally. She confirmed my fears and, knowing my sense of humour, said jokingly, 'You are either pregnant or you will need a hysterectomy.' I was a new grandmother at the time!

Very quickly, wheels were set in motion. After surgery, I was treated for ovarian cancer, with all the associated physical and emotional traumas. This time the poem ministered to me.

We had enjoyed thirty wonderful years in Suffolk, raising our four daughters, but the time had come to move on. In October that year, coinciding with the end of my chemotherapy and following two years of prayerful planning, we moved to Surrey to be closer to our daughters and their families. The God of time and circumstance led us into a new life, brave amid the sadness of leaving our friends behind.

Since then the Lord has reinvested his poem many times, using it to encourage new friends facing life-changing circumstances. The words have given them peace and comfort during times of waiting.

I have now renamed the poem, 'Tears of the Heart'.

You might like to use Jan's poem as a prayer, for yourself or for someone you love.

Tears of the Heart

O Lord, when I am crying in my heart
and no one sees but you,
when I hide secret, doubtful thoughts,
so they won't filter through;
collect my tears,
and use them for the healing
of my fears.

Take my imagination that would rob
my days of hopeful joy.

Waiting on God

Let me remember all the things
you promise to supply.
Your love so kind,
will shatter fear and give me
peace of mind.

O Lord, the sunshine comes and goes, as does
the rain from day to day
and glorious shines the rainbow when
the storm has passed away.
For only you
can see the sunlight hidden
from my view.

And I trust you, Lord.

After waiting

Do you know the one about the keen Christian who, having drowned in a flood, arrived at the pearly gates and treated St Peter to a good old grumble?

'I stood at my window as my front room flooded,' he complained. 'A man in waders came by and offered to help me to safety. I laughed. "Don't worry about me, the Lord will provide. There are others far more in need."

'Later, as dirty water lapped at my stairs, I retreated to my bedroom. A man rowed past. "Climb in, Granddad!"

' "No, no, very kind of you but the Lord will provide. Help my neighbours instead."

'The waters rose still further and I struggled out of the bedroom window to perch on my roof. A helicopter hovered overhead – what a noise it made. Soon an air–sea rescue fellow was dangling on a rope above me, but I wouldn't go with him.

'The Bible says that the Lord will rescue those who call upon him, but I waited and waited and he never came.'

St Peter laughed. 'He sent a man in waders, one in a boat and several in a helicopter,' he said. 'What more did you expect?'

* * *

Sun of righteousness

For you who revere my name, the sun of righteousness will rise
with healing in its wings. And you will go out and leap like calves
released from the stall.   (Malachi 4.2)

Adjusting even to the joyous outcome of a period of waiting may
mean a time when we need more than ever to keep pace with
the Lord. Waiting can make people worse as well as better – think
of Noah who waited out the promise of rain, the flood itself
and the encouraging growth of a vineyard from scratch, only
to become drunk and nearly ruin everything.

When Malachi's words were written, Israel awaited a
Messiah to save her from corruption and rule over her with
righteousness. Jesus (which means Saviour) Christ (a Greek
word which in Hebrew is 'Messiah', in English 'Anointed One')
arrived 400 years later, but few recognized him and 'leapt'
for joy. Most failed to see, let alone adjust to the post-waiting
era. And even for those who did respond the waiting continued – he had been anointed and equipped to save, showing the way to righteousness, justice, love and mercy but
not everyone chose to follow him. That's why we too are still
waiting.

Recently someone explained to me the imagery in this verse.
Cattle are kept indoors all winter. On the spring day when
they are released into the great grassy spaces, lumbering cows
really do leap for joy, even the grandmas among them. Their
calves, knowing only the dark confinement of cowsheds where
they were born, have never imagined anything so good, just as
we cannot begin to imagine the freedom, light, space, feasting
and joy of heaven.

If heaven's that good, why has God kept us waiting two thousand years? June Newcombe, from drystone-wall territory in

the north of England, wrote a psalm-like piece which suggests the underlying reason as God's mercy. His healing may come quick as a sunrise but often – even with someone as righteous as Noah – it takes time. (To explain, from what I remember of O-level geography an 'erratic' is a boulder which has been carved out and carried along by a glacier so that it no longer matches the geology of its new resting place.)

My God is a drystone waller

Watch the drystone waller at work surrounded by rocks.
He chooses:
the jagged and carefully shapes it;
the smooth, which needs little work and which he loves to
     use;
the boulder, which needs all his strength to work with;
the erratic which is out of place and doesn't fit in;
the pebble, so insignificant, but for which he has a special
     use –
And out of these he fashions a wall exactly right for his
     purpose.

My God is a drystone waller.
He chooses:
the jagged – the harsh, the unkind, the unfeeling and chips
     away at its rough edges;
the smooth – the beautiful, the endearing, the bringer of joy,
     which he polishes until he sees his reflection;
the boulder – the dominating, the self-important, which
     requires a special skill;
the erratic – the eccentric, the misfit and knows just how to
     use it;
he chooses the pebble – the unimportant, the worthless and
     gently places it in the gaps to hold all the rest together;
they all take their place in the wall,

a strong wall built with love and skill for protection and
   defence –
God's wall lasts for ever but always needs renewing.

* * *

Get what you wanted?

Women received back their dead, raised to life again. Others
were tortured and refused to be released, so that they might
gain a better resurrection. Some faced jeers and flogging, while
still others were chained and put in prison. They were stoned;
they were sawn in two; they were put to death by the sword.
They went about in sheepskins and goatskins, destitute, per-
secuted and ill-treated – the world was not worthy of them.
They wandered in deserts and mountains, and in caves and holes
in the ground. These were all commended for their faith, yet
none of them received what had been promised.

(Hebrews 11.35–39)

Looking back over history, Hebrews 11 tells of the great Jewish
heroes of faith, all of whom were 'longing for a better country –
a heavenly one' (verse 16). Some of them saw amazing things
happen: others suffered hugely. All died without 'receiving
what had been promised' – and longed for.

Jesus came to earth, died and rose again, yet God's will is
still not always 'done on earth as it is in heaven'. Partly because
some human beings go on choosing evil, sadly some people
will never receive what they have been promised in this life.
Looking back, some would say they had received other bless-
ings which have brought light, hope for the future, a new start
perhaps. Often God transforms what had seemed a hopelessly
messy mixture of a lot of evil and a little good into a different
pattern, where love and goodness can begin to thrive again.

After waiting

Dorrith Sim lives in Ayrshire, though I met her on holiday in Crete. Evil destroyed her parents – but here she writes about new beginnings.

It was 9 November 1938, in Germany. My Jewish school had been wrecked that morning.

'There'll be more trouble,' Vati (Daddy) foretold. 'We must take some children from the *Weisenhaus* (the Jewish orphanage) home with us.'

That night, *Kristallnacht* (the Night of the Broken Glass), the Nazis tramped up our stairs. They did much damage and took my father away. God must have been with us for Vati returned the next day and the children from the *Weisenhaus* were spared the lighted petrol bombs which had been thrown through their orphanage windows.

My parents wanted to keep me free from danger. A scheme called *Kindertransport* was being set up for unaccompanied children, mainly Jewish, to come to the UK. Now we had to wait for my documents before I would be allowed to travel. Mutti (Mummy) got my case ready. With everything else she packed two photograph albums to remind me of happier times.

It was July 1939 before my papers arrived. I was seven and a half. Mutti and Vati travelled with me to Hamburg Railway Station which was awash with children, many crying. Parents were not allowed on the platform. Soon the train moved off on its journey to Holland.

A boat waited to ship us to Harwich. From there we boarded a train for London's Liverpool Street Station. Many people were waiting for the children's arrival. A couple approached me. 'Dorrith?' they asked.

At seven and a half I answered in the only English I knew. 'I have a handkerchief in my pocket.'

My new guardians lived in Edinburgh. They were good to me but I missed my parents. My guardians arranged their passage to Scotland but it was too late. The war began on 3 September 1939.

I stayed with Fred and Sophie Gallimore until November 1952. Their own family, Rosalind and Elizabeth, were born in 1942 and 1947.

I waited and waited for word of my parents, Hans and Trudi Oppenheim, and prayed that they would be safe. When the news came through I wouldn't believe it. They'd been sent to Theresienstadt and then to Auschwitz concentration camps.

Where was God in all this? I can't answer except to give thanks for the family he allowed me to have – for those to whom I'm Mum, Gran or Great-Gran. How proud my parents would have been of them all. Fred, Sophie and Elizabeth are no longer with us. Happily Rosalind now continues as a very close member of our family.

Almost ten thousand mainly Jewish children were welcomed into the UK before World War II broke out. Over the years, Dorrith has helped organize reunions for former *Kindertransport* children as well as ex-refugees and camp survivors who settled in Scotland. When Dorrith told her story to a group of seventy British guests at a Christian hotel in Crete, she could hardly believe it when one lady exclaimed, 'But this is my story too. I was a *Kindertransport* child!' What horrors and yet what rescues; what evil and yet what kindness from strangers, many of whom took these children into their own homes.

Lord, when we hear stories like this, our own grumbles about waiting seem so petty. Millions today wait through war, famine, slavery, oppression . . . Help us to hear the cries of those who, like those German Jewish parents in 1939, are waiting in utter desperation. Help us to reach out in kindness wherever we can, to bring hope and a new start.

* * *

The twists and turns of 'being found'

But while he was still a long way off, his father saw him and was filled with compassion for him; he ran to his son, threw his arms around him and kissed him.

The son said to him, 'Father, I have sinned against heaven and against you. I am no longer worthy to be called your son.'

But the father said to his servants, 'Quick! Bring the best robe and put it on him. Put a ring on his finger and sandals on his feet. Bring the fattened calf and kill it. Let's have a feast and celebrate. For this son of mine was dead and is alive again; he was lost and is found.' So they began to celebrate.

Meanwhile . . . the older brother became angry and refused to go in. So his father went out and pleaded with him.

But he answered his father, 'Look! All these years I've been slaving for you and never disobeyed your orders. Yet you never gave me even a young goat so I could celebrate with my friends. But when this son of yours who has squandered your property with prostitutes comes home, you kill the fattened calf for him!'

'My son,' the father said, 'you are always with me, and everything I have is yours. But we had to celebrate and be glad, because this brother of yours was dead and is alive again; he was lost and is found.'   (Luke 15.20–32)

I've known my friend Roma since we were at university together. Not so long ago she arranged a holiday to St Petersburg primarily in order to spend time gazing at Rembrandt's painting of the prodigal son in the Hermitage Museum there. She remained staring at it for so long that her husband feared that she'd be arrested – but the reason for her interest was not to steal it, nor even that she particularly liked it or had some great interest in art. Rather that on a previous holiday she'd been so impacted by preaching on the 'prodigal son' that she knew that God had more to say to her. The preacher had referred often to Henri Nouwen's book which is based on Rembrandt's picture. She read the book and made that long pilgrimage to see the picture which Rembrandt painted at the end of his life, when he was nearly blind and destitute but had made rich discoveries about his relationship with God.

The reason why, in God's economy, Roma made this particular journey will become clearer when you read the story of what happened afterwards – she's told it in her own words below. But first do read Jesus' familiar parable right through, thinking about what it says about the Father waiting for us to find our true identity in him. The son who cut himself off and chased after bright lights returned to find an unexpected welcome as his father's son. The older son who stayed was, at the end of the story, ambivalent about his own place in the family, despite his father's assurance that 'everything I have is yours'. Before embarking on anything much, we're wise to seek that assurance of being family, that 'I am his and he is mine'. If Roma had not, from the depths of her being, found the truth of that from her heavenly Father, things might well have worked out very differently for her.

Here is Roma's story:

A long while ago I heard a phrase which impacted me deeply. It was, 'If you know, you don't need to think about it any more.' It's so *true*!

Until I made contact with my father there was scarcely a day in my fifty-four years when I didn't think about him. I was born illegitimate, brought up mainly by my grandmother until I was eleven, when I went to live with my mother and stepfather. Family relationships were strained. Anything to do with feelings was taboo – so was my genetic father. All I gleaned was that he was an Italian doctor at Moorfields Eye

Hospital where my mother worked – and that his surname, Ferrari, was my middle name. After my grandmother died twenty years ago my mother let slip once that he was married, planned to divorce and marry her, changed his mind, got back with his wife and, shortly after I was born, emigrated to Canada. A solicitor tried to trace him for maintenance for me, but couldn't.

I grew up, graduated, married, became a teacher; I had four sons and a good life. Yet scarcely a day went by when I didn't think about my father, either fantasizing – building him up to almost the status of a god, or despairing – he'd abandoned me and it wasn't my fault. When my mother died suddenly I felt so sad that I would never know the truth about him. My uncle and aunt in Cornwall were the only others who might have any information, but from them I learned just one new fact, his first name – Raymo. I tried, and failed, to trace him.

Not long afterwards, at a new neighbour's drinks party I found myself chatting with a man called Peter who said he was a private investigator. 'What do you investigate?' I asked.

'I find lost mummies and daddies.' Peter agreed to search on my behalf and eventually traced a doctor in Canada called Remo (not Raymo) Ferrari. Next day Peter called, 'I've spoken to your father on the phone. He acknowledges you and has no problem with your phoning him.'

It was the hardest phone call I have ever made. I hoped just to hear his voice, acknowledging me as his daughter – that would have given me the connection that I have always longed for. But the phone call gave me so much more – he was warm, friendly, glad I'd made contact, had a sense of humour, asked questions and showed an interest in me and my family. He told me that he was eighty-three, had two sons and two daughters in Canada and, apart from very poor sight and arthritis, was well. He wanted to keep in contact and invited my whole family to visit him in Vancouver. I wanted to jump on a plane the next day, but he was about to stay with his daughter.

I'd like to say the story ended happily ever after but when he returned, he didn't want to know me any more. I've no idea why – maybe his family advised him against it. At first I was upset but then I thought, I'd wanted to hear his voice but I had far more than that.

A few weeks later a supply teacher I've known for years but not seen for a while came rushing up to me at work. 'I've been dying to know, how did it go when you went to see your father?'

I explained what had happened. Her face dropped. 'I'm so sorry!' It was then that I realized that for several weeks I'd not thought about my father at all. My story had reached its conclusion. Even though it had turned out very differently from what I had hoped, I felt a real peace, strength and happiness and I knew the outcome was the best possible. Since then many people who have known me for years have remarked that I'm a completely different person – that I now have belief in myself and have come alive.

Some of us have far from perfect impressions of fatherhood – maybe that's why we wait years to know you as our loving Father, or to find our identity in your family. Help us to get to know you, as the runaway son and Roma came to know you; help us to see that our life is now hidden with Christ in God (Colossians 3.3).

* * *

Reflections: looking forward, glancing back

I have been deprived of peace; I have forgotten what prosperity is. So I say, 'My splendour is gone and all that I had hoped from the LORD.' . . . My soul is downcast within me. Yet this I call to mind and therefore I have hope: Because of the LORD's great love we are not consumed, for his compassions never fail. They are new every morning; great is your faithfulness. I say to myself, 'The LORD is my portion; therefore I will wait for him.' The LORD is good to those whose hope is in him, to the one who seeks him; it is good to wait quietly for the salvation of the LORD . . . For men are not cast off by the Lord for ever. Though he brings grief, he will show compassion, so great is his unfailing love. For he does not willingly bring affliction or grief to the children of men . . . I called on your name, O LORD, from the depths of the pit. You heard my plea: 'Do not close your ears to my cry for relief.' You came near when I called you, and you said, 'Do not fear.' O Lord, you took up my case; you redeemed my life.

(Lamentations 3.17–26, 31–33, 55–58)

After all the promises and all their journeyings with God, which involved plenty of waits along the road, Israel had gone into exile. God was using the experience to purify them and to restore their relationship with himself. That didn't make it any less painful at the time but they did have hope. They looked back in sadness and regret – it could have all been so different – but they could also look forward as they waited in a foreign land. Maybe they had what they needed at that time, if not what they wanted – nor what, in the original plan, God had wanted for them.

How do we feel, looking back on our lives – and looking forward into the future? Maybe it takes a time of quiet waiting before we even think to take stock in this way. If we're in one of those uncomfortable waiting times and the future seems bleak, do we find hope in God as the writer of Lamentations did? Perhaps we see what we've learned? Patience? If we look through God's eyes, maybe our 'splendour' is not gone but is being enhanced!

Eric Leat, a retired accountant in his eighties, wrote this telling poem from the point of view of a mirror reflecting the life of a woman.

Mirror

For sixty years no day has passed
Without her pausing just to glance
My way and sometimes talk to me.
A child, it was on tip of toe
She first saw me, and saw herself.
So pretty, pert and trying to
Look older than her seven years.
And then at ten she told herself,
(Not knowing I was listening),
She did not care about these things
Like prettiness and such, and boys;
But still she could not pass me by
Without a glance, without a smile.

At twelve she blossomed beautifully:
She looked me fully in the face,
No more pretence of carelessness.
And so she grew in charm and grace.
Sometimes there would be men with her
So close to her, kissing her ear,
Stroking her hair, making her laugh.
Then on her wedding day her face
Was pale but I could see the joy
And see determination too.
I'm glad she chose the quiet one.

When children came, two boys, a girl,
Reflection time was all too short,
But I was not forgotten then,

After waiting

For not a day without a look
And often lifting high a child
For me to see and to be seen.

Years passed, the children found their way.
I'd see them, sometimes, visiting,
But when they left she looked at me
And knew that she faced loneliness,
Her husband dead, her children gone

And yesterday she smiled and said:
'I'll have to learn to be like you,
Patient; hanging there in the hall
Waiting, with your back to the wall.'

Eric was himself facing a difficult and dangerous operation not long ago and did some stocktaking as he waited with his back against the wall. He'd lost his wife to cancer a year or so before, yet those who went to cheer him came away encouraged and with their own faith built up because of the very real way in which his faith shone through. He writes:

The doctor says: 'I'm afraid the news is not good.' You know what he means. After weeks of tests and scans and consultations the operation. They told me afterwards that it was the biggest cancer operation they do at the Royal Marsden Hospital; it took nine hours followed by ten days in the Critical Care Unit. For most of this time I could not even speak as a tracheotomy was in place and I was strictly a 'nil by mouth' case – not even a drip of water.

The unexpected thing was that while I was physically so weak I felt spiritually strong, closer to God than I had ever been: amazing grace indeed. I could not read, write or speak, but the one thing I could do was to pray and, poor as my prayers may have been, they were from the depths.

This feeling of nearness to God does not take away the pain, the weakness, the frustration, but it does take away the anxiety, the fear, the doubting. God was with me, loving me – tough love indeed – I have described it as going through a deep, dark place and I believe I'm the better person for having been on this journey.

Spend some time reflecting and 'stocktaking' with God.

* * *

After waiting: learning to keep pace, to 'dance' with him

Not running ahead or falling behind

Philip went down to a city in Samaria and proclaimed the Christ . . . there was great joy in that city . . .

Now an angel of the Lord said to Philip, 'Go south to the road – the desert road – that goes down from Jerusalem to Gaza.'

So he started out, and on his way he met an Ethiopian eunuch, an important official in charge of all the treasury of Candace, queen of the Ethiopians. This man had gone to Jerusalem to worship, and on his way home was sitting in his chariot reading the book of Isaiah the prophet. The Spirit told Philip, 'Go to that chariot and stay near it.'

. . . Philip began with that very passage of Scripture and told him the good news about Jesus . . .

Philip baptised him. When they came up out of the water, the Spirit of the Lord suddenly took Philip away, and the eunuch did not see him again, but went on his way rejoicing. Philip, however, appeared at Azotus and travelled about, preaching the gospel in all the towns until he reached Caesarea.

(Taken from Acts 8.5–40)

The disciples waited in Jerusalem after Jesus' ascension, until the Holy Spirit came upon them – and then the action kept heating up. So I wonder what Philip felt when an angel of the Lord, no less, told him to leave a place where he'd started a real revival and journey to some lonely desert road? That hardly seems logical and it doesn't look as if the angel explained the reason. Philip's next instruction came when he saw the chariot. Then, perhaps, it all started to make sense. If Philip led this one particular man to meet Jesus, he, being an influential person in his own country, might go on to evangelize many Africans.

Philip's next step, explaining the gospel, would have come naturally to an evangelist – but after he baptizes the Ethiopian he experiences a 'beam me up, Scotty' moment. Suddenly and inexplicably, he's off evangelizing towns in other parts.

Keeping pace with the Spirit isn't easy for mere mortals. Personal instructions from angels, let alone some form of supernatural tele-transportation don't fall within most people's experience. Would we cope if they did?

What is the Lord asking you and me to do? Does he want us to stop, proceed slowly, jump in, wait for others or steam ahead? We don't want to be presumptuous, running faster than he desires – nor to be left behind. Sometimes, though we think we've heard right, the instructions seem so odd. When we've done the equivalent of talking to one individual on a road to nowhere, the reason why hasn't become as clear as it was to Philip. So we wait, walk and even run blind. Only looking back perhaps do we come to see the whys and wherefores. Like the writer, Veronica Heley, who tells the story of how her life's work ground to a halt:

For some years I had all my ideas for books accepted by publishers and had gone from contract to contract without any trouble at all. I was on a roll and life was good. I'd stopped writing the historical romances which used to do so well in the libraries but almost immediately started filling a much-needed niche with Christian fiction for children. I was often asked into schools to talk, run workshops, even lead assemblies.

Meanwhile the Association of Christian Writers asked several times if I'd go on their committee and eventually it seemed I could just about fit it into my busy life, so I accepted. And my work dried up, just like that. For the first time for many years none of the ideas I put forward to publishers made it to contract stage, and publishers didn't have any ideas for me, either.

I was a writer with nothing to write. I continued to put forward ideas for books, I continued to write reviews and the occasional article for magazines, but nothing gelled in the way of a book contract.

I was desperate. What had gone wrong? Yes, some editors had changed jobs, or their guidelines had been changed. Perhaps the fault was in me? I'd been getting published for twenty years by that time. Perhaps I'd lost my touch, and should consider myself well and truly out of date?

Meanwhile, the work for the Fellowship of Christian Writers (as it was then) became a burden of a different kind. God encouraged me to apply for one of the hardest jobs on the committee, that of events organizer. It seemed to me he was saying, 'This is the time for you to give something back to others.' So I tried to help other writers to become more professional, and to create opportunities for them to contact publishers and editors. Somehow or other we ran the first ACW weekend, and our numbers grew. It wasn't the same as being a writer. Oh, no! It certainly wasn't. I did so miss being a writer.

When my term of office came to a close, I was exhausted, relieved and more than ready to pass the buck to someone else. At that point the most amazing thing happened: two publishers asked me to write for them. One wanted a straightforward biography of St Paul. (What, me? I'm no theologian, said I. Ah, but you're a storyteller, they said, and that's what we want.) The other wanted a series of murder mysteries with a Christian background which was to go not only into Christian bookshops, but also into the secular ones . . . which later led on to my being asked to write a romance/suspense series for an American Christian publisher as well. Most recently, my secular publisher asked for another series and, on seeing my draft, wondered if I could make it 'a bit more Christian'!

Ten years and twenty more books after it all ground to a halt, I continue to marvel at how God steered me this way and that. I didn't want to stop writing for the years I was on the committee, but I can see now why he wanted me to do something else for a while, and I thank and praise him for the way he opened up new opportunities for writing when I'd done as he asked.

Veronica's recent books include:

The Ellie Quicke Mysteries: HarperCollins & Severn House
The *Eden Hall* series: Zondervan
Who, Me? Paul Stories of Everyday Saints, BRF
New series *The Abbot Agency*. No 1 *False Charity*. Severn House. 2007 onwards

Lord, when we feel as if we're partnering you in some dance that we don't know, in time to music we can't hear, help us to stay close to you and trust you, through all the stops and starts, the quicks and slows, the leaps and tiptoes. Help us to wait on you!

* * *

Steadfast and faithful

Have mercy on me, O God, have mercy on me, for in you my soul takes refuge. I will take refuge in the shadow of your wings until the disaster has passed. I cry out to God Most High, to God, who fulfils his purpose for me. He sends from heaven and saves me, rebuking those who hotly pursue me; *Selah*. God sends his love and his faithfulness. They spread a net for my feet – I was bowed down in distress. They dug a pit in my path – but they have fallen into it themselves. *Selah*. My heart is steadfast, O God, my heart is steadfast; I will sing and make music. Awake, my soul! Awake, harp and lyre! I will awaken the dawn. I will praise you, O Lord, among the nations; I will sing of you among the peoples. For great is your love, reaching to the heavens; your faithfulness reaches to the skies. Be exalted, O God, above the heavens; let your glory be over all the earth.

(Psalm 57.1–11)

The psalmist appears to be on a roller coaster, lurching to panic, soaring to trust – then down and up he goes again. I identify with that. I may find peace with God in the midst of a difficult situation – but in the enforced wait, lose that peace again. It's good to remind myself then that God is not in a panic, nor swooping wildly between extremes of emotions. Have you noticed the interesting little word in many of the psalms which perhaps gives a clue as to how to tap into God's peace and stead-fastness? *Selah*. It occurs twice above and means, roughly, 'Be quiet a minute and let that sink in' (literally 'rest' – a term used in music today). Bearing in mind that the psalms were sung in worship, I can imagine the musicians continuing to play for a few moments while the congregation stops singing and lets their spirits realign themselves to God's. Often the sung words, when they begin again, have changed emotion – they're still honest but in pace with divine rather than human thought, will and feeling. Notice this is not so much about individuals as a body of worshippers – a congregation's complex roller coaster.

Many different kinds of musical instruments took part in Jewish worship – which interests me because I've been thinking about the idea of waiting in relation to an orchestra. Not all instruments play at once. Maybe the flute has many bars, even pages, of rests – and then comes in, fresh and bright. I do think any church is a bit like that – if Jesus is conducting he won't necessarily want all the instruments playing at once. The fact that you or I have a time of waiting, of 'rests', at the moment isn't a sign that we're redundant – in fact it's really important that we don't bash our drums in the middle of the quiet bit with the harp and piccolo. I'm just old enough to remember an oft-repeated TV sketch which used an early form of trick photography to show the comedian Charlie Drake playing every instrument in the orchestra – rows of trombones keeping time, of violins fiddling and so on. Every so often the camera would fix on a lone triangle player, counting the bars for his one moment of glory – 2,467 . . . 2,468 . . . Poor man, it never came. We on the other hand do have to trust that Jesus will bring us in at the right time. Perhaps then we'll be playing a short but noisy spectacular, all by ourselves. After that we must wait again with our hearts steadfast, our ears listening to the rhythms and harmonies of the other players and our eyes fixed on our conductor.

I spoke with Geoff Tothill, who at ninety-three is the oldest member of my church. He's worshipped there for thirty-seven years, has spent a lifetime following Jesus and is one of those Christians who give the rest of us a good name. He says himself that he's never done anything spectacular, never set the world alight. He's been a widower for many years and at his

141

age various physical disabilities mean that he can't do very much at all – but it's evident that his heart is steadfast – he's a real rock in our midst. Geoff is never dogmatic but we can all see that here is a man who knows God, through life's ups and downs – and who always seeks to love, include and encourage others. 'I'm not an upfront person, not a preacher,' he said. 'I'm a Barnabas really, a helper, an encourager.'

Our church has paid clergy. Lay leaders also serve for a set number of years before they must hand the baton on to someone else. I think this is healthy for the life of the church but individuals often struggle when they come off leadership. I asked Geoff, who had been a leader, how he coped.

'It wasn't easy,' he said.

> One minute you're at the hub of everything, in touch with everyone – and then you're almost on the fringe. People don't take so much notice of what you say. And then of course human beings don't always like change but churches do change over the years – often because God wants them to change. I think God's been gentle with our church – brought in change gradually. But whatever happens you can still love people, encourage them, welcome strangers. I can still do those things, even at my age, now I've given up my own home and moved to sheltered accommodation. I think I have a happy spirit and that's of the Lord. I can be a quiet witness to his goodness where I live, in church, with my family – children, grandchildren and great-grandchildren.

Geoff spoke a great deal about being thankful – you could say his quieter years have become a thankful *Selah*.

> I'm thankful for a number of godly men from my youth who taught me well – although in those days they were a bit rigid, it was a good foundation. Later, the Holy Spirit filled me with

love for people and with worship. He's also sent various people into my life who've become like family to me – like brothers, even though our ages are quite different and even though my own brother died some years ago. I've had one or two regular prayer partners, that's been a tremendous strength and due to many people's faithful, ongoing care and fellowship, at ninety-three my life is different but not too difficult.

At my funeral I want the reading to be from Philippians 4. I've sought to live by those verses. They are so practical – and I've proved that they work!

You might like to meditate on those verses yourself:

> Rejoice in the Lord always. I will say it again: Rejoice!
> Let your gentleness be evident to all. The Lord is near.
> Do not be anxious about anything, but in everything, by prayer and petition, with thanksgiving, present your requests to God.
> And the peace of God, which transcends all understanding, will guard your hearts and your minds in Christ Jesus.
> Finally, brothers, whatever is true, whatever is noble, whatever is right, whatever is pure, whatever is lovely, whatever is admirable – if anything is excellent or praiseworthy – think about such things . . .
> I have learned to be content whatever the circumstances.
> I know what it is to be in need, and I know what it is to have plenty. I have learned the secret of being content in any and every situation, whether well fed or hungry, whether living in plenty or in want.
> I can do everything through him who gives me strength.
>
> (Philippians 4.4–8, 11–13)

*   *   *

I AM

health for your bones
honey to your lips
balm on your feet
light to your eyes
perfumed oil on your skin
cool water for your throat
wine to warm your belly
salt on your tongue
a song in your ears
warmth all over;
a rhythm for your heart
breath in your lungs
strength for your knees
power to your arm
a dance in your life
peace for your brain, your pain,
glory instead of shame.
And you may
drink me, eat me, live me, now, always.